PHARMA PACKAGING INNOVATIONS

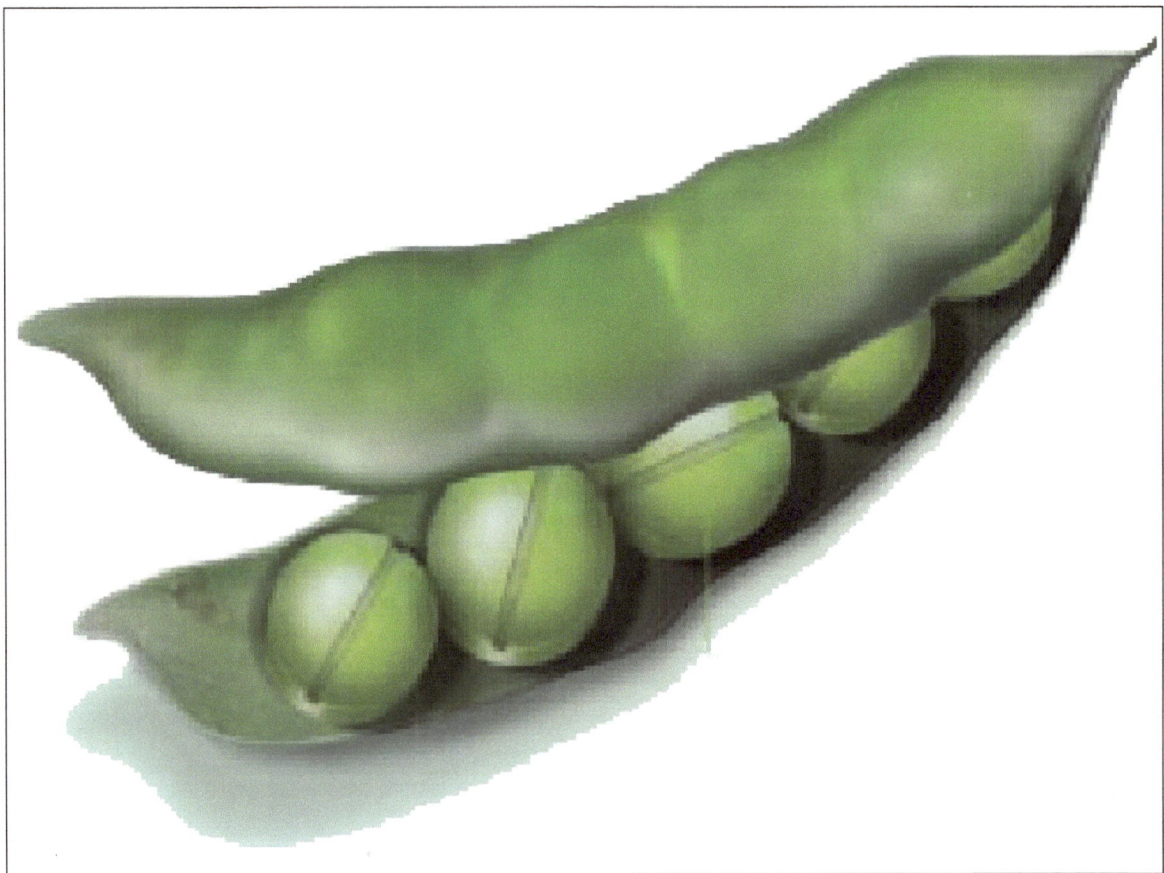

PHARMA PACKAGING INNOVATIONS

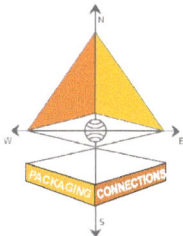

Sanex Packaging Connections Pvt. Ltd.
www.packagingconnections.com

Copyright

Published by :

Sanex Packaging Connections Pvt. Ltd.

An ISO 9001 : 2008 Certified Organisation

117, Suncity Tower, Sector-54

Golf Course Road, Gurgoan-122 002.

Tel : +91 124 4965770

Fax : + 91 124 41433951

e-mail : info@packagingconnections.com

Like us on Facebook : www.facebook.com/pconnection

ISBN : 978-8192792033

List of Contributors

Team www.PackagingConnections.com by Sanex Packaging Connections Pvt Ltd

Sandeep Kumar Goyal, Founder & CEO
Amita Venkatesh Vallesha, Associate: Scientific Affairs & Consultancy
Chhavi Aggarwal, Associate: Research & Business Consulting
Bhaskar Ch, Technology Advisor e-business
Sonu Sheoran, Associate Research & Technology
Ashok Kumar, Programme Manager: KPO

Table of Contents

Introduction by Sandeep Kumar Goyal 10

Pharmaceutical Design...**12-45**

Sphereon 14-15

E-Z-LinkTM Vial Adapter 15-17

Compliance Packaging 16-19

Interactive Slider Pack...20-21

Sominex 22-23

Trial Pack in unique shape 24-25

Vaccject 26-27

Child Resistant Dispensing Pack 28-29

AirShield™ Tube 30-31

CR Overcap – Bottom Lock...32-33

CR Overcap – Top Lock 34-35

Pill storage and water 36-37

Auto Drop & Auto Squeeze 38-39

Infant formula tub with AccuMeasure scoop 40-41

Med-Easy 42-43

Dispensing Closure 44-45

Pharmaceutical Break Through................................**46-63**

Pill Dispenser...48-49

Multi-Compartment Pockets 50-51

Stick Packs 52-53

Desiccant Bottles 54-55

Roll On Ball for Baby powder 56-57

Chiller for VET vaccines 58-59

Senior Friendly Closures 60-61

Single Serve Bottles by Compression Molding................62-63

Pharmaceutical Value Engineering **64-69**

Contact Lens Packaging..66-67

Material Shift (Glass to Plastic).......................................68-69

Pharmaceutical Compliance Packaging **71-79**

Electronic Compliance Monitor 72-73

Textured Caps..74-75

Colour Coding 76-77

Quick Release Pack 78-79

Pharmaceutical Technology **80-101**

Syringe Adapter...82-83

Zeo Cool 84-85

Green Box 86-87

Child Resistant Tube Closure 88-89

Smart Braille Solution 90-91

Dry Keep - Desiccant 92-93

Vented Induction Liner 94-95

Micro Mixer 96-97

Oligodynamic Components 98-99

High Barrier Compression Molding Technology.............100-101

Pharmaceutical Concepts....................................**102-111**

Independent Remedies 104-105

Tetrahedron Tablet Packaging 106-107

Chameleon Bandages 108-109

ClearRx 110-111

Pharmaceutical Anti - Counterfeiting..................**112-123**

Security Solutions...114-115

Folding Box Temper Evidence 116-117

Impact Resistance by Label 118-119

SHR Packaging 120-121

Pharma Comb Void Labels 122-123

Thank you..124

PHARMA PACKAGING INNOVATIONS

Introduction

This publication comes after the success of Ideas & Opportunities 2013 held on 19th July 2013 in India. Various innovations were presented during the one day workshop by the expert consulting team of Sanex packaging Connections Pvt Ltd popularly known as Team PackagingConnections.

Idea behind this is to bring the innovations to wider group of professionals to meet the mission of packaging knowledge sharing and that too cost effectively. We feel that this publication will further fill the project pipelines of companies and improve the standards of packaging. Many professionals either do not have the access or time to go through so many innovations together. So we think this publication will fill that gap. For your feedback please email directly to info@packagingconnections.com

With this, Enjoy Wonders Of Packaging!

Sandeep Kumar Goyal
Founder & CEO ,
www.PackagingConnections.com

Pharmaceutical

Design

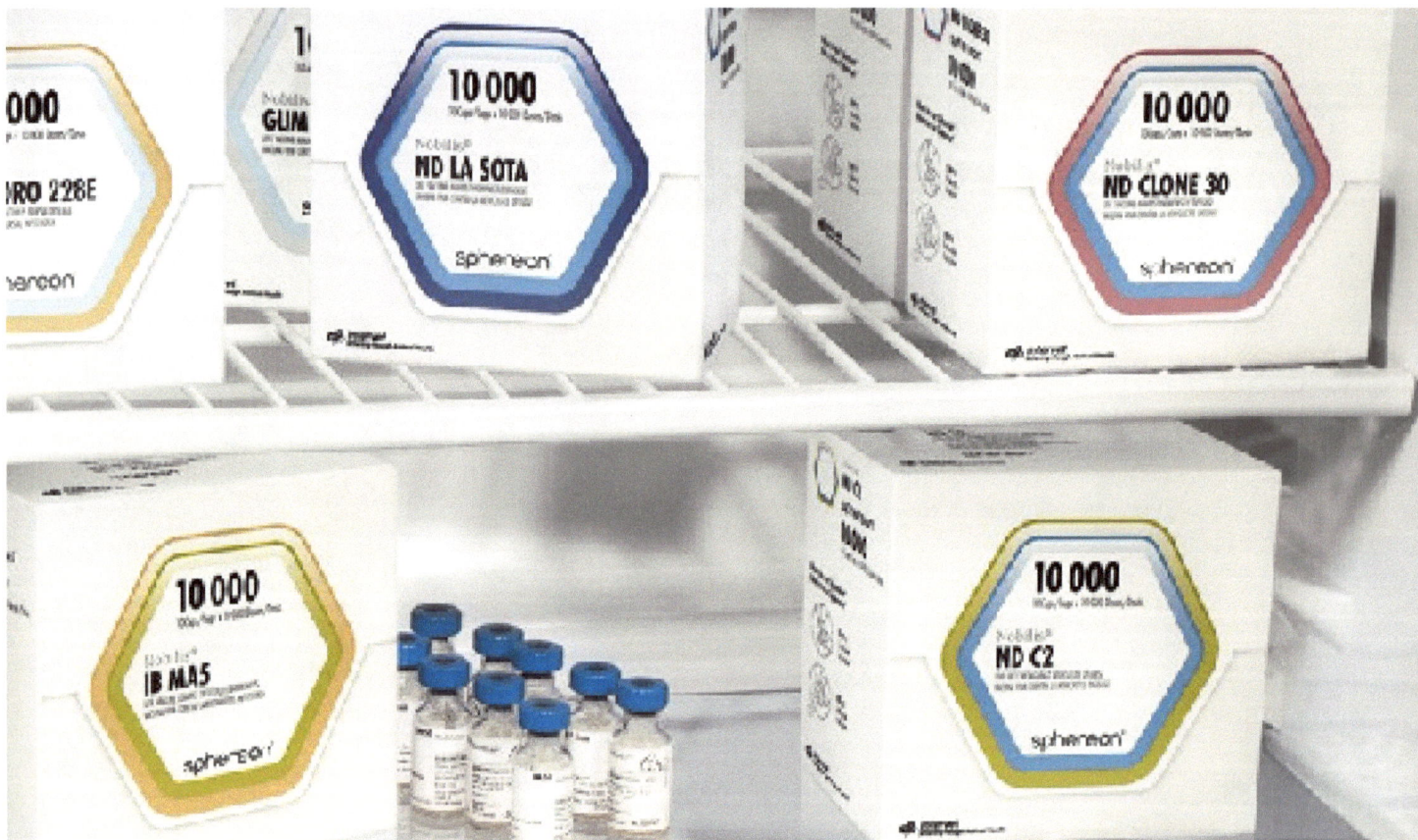

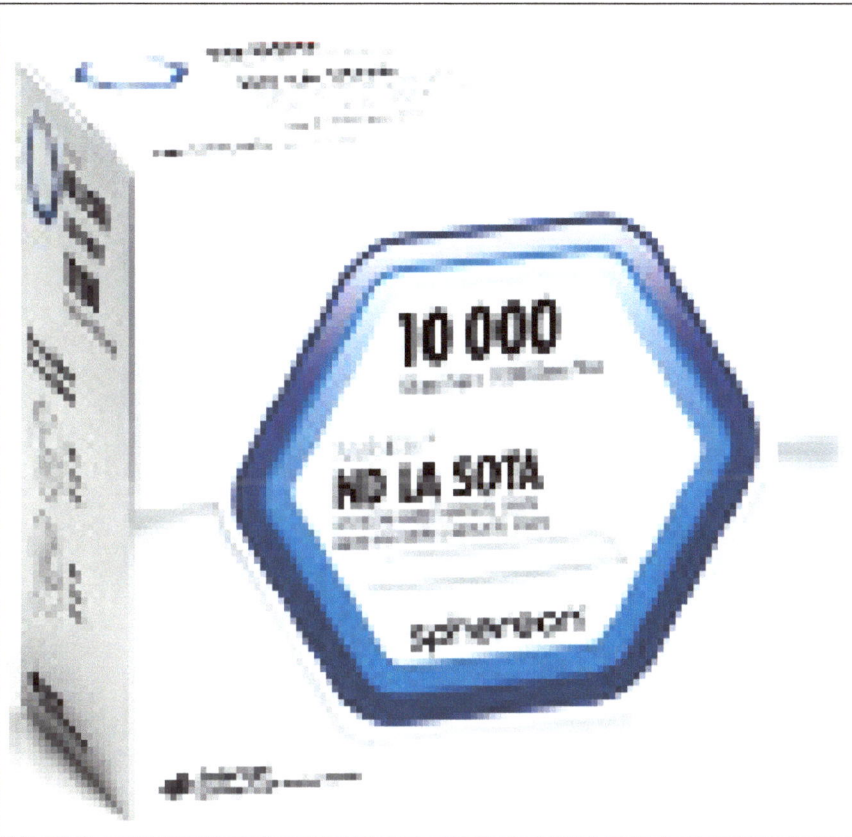

Manufacturer/Designer

Design Bridge London
18 Clerkenwell Design Bridge
London
18 Clerkenwell CloseLondon
EC1R 0QN United Kingdom
T: +44 (0)20 7814 9922
F: +44 (0)20 7814 9024
Email: sales_london@designbridge.com"

- The 'Protective Hexagon', user-friendly 2D and 3D pack designs.

- The hexagon icon is a powerful visual equity that colour codes with ease

- To create a crystal clear range architecture, eliminating error and confusion.

- With a name inspired by the new, spherical vaccine pills.

- Can be thermoformed

- Can then eliminate bottles and do in house thermoforming to save cost

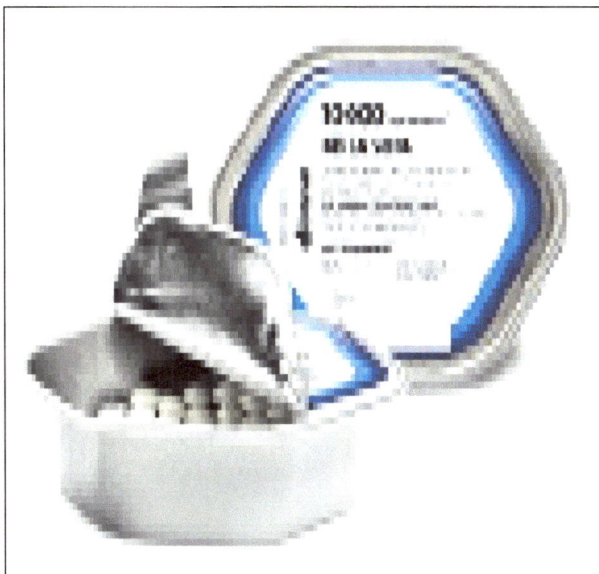

Manufacturer/Designer

DUOJECT MEDICAL SYSTEMS INC.
50 CHEMIN DE GASPÉ, COMPLEX B-5
BROMONT (QUEBEC) CANADA
J2L 2N8
T: 877-534-3666
F: 450-534-3700
Email: E-NOVATIONS@DUOJECT.COM

Needle based Vial Adapter for reconstitution of solid form drugs in standard drug vials

Integrated safety feature – needle never exposed before or after reconstitution

Diluent in standard syringe with luer-lock tip

Compatible with wide range of syringe sizes

Compatible with 13mm or 20mm finish drug vials

Sequential activation

Single use device

PHARMA PACKAGING INNOVATIONS

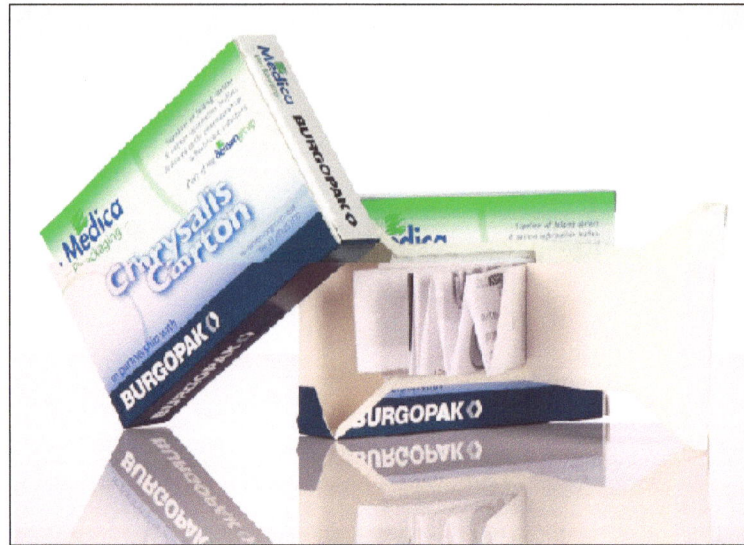

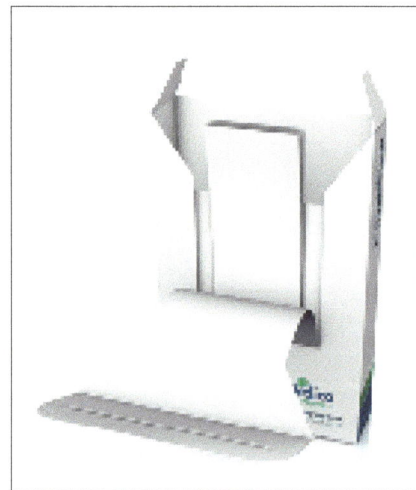

PHARMA PACKAGING INNOVATIONS

Manufacturer/Designer

Burgopak Germany Ltd.
Alexandrinenstraße 2-3 Aufgang C
10969 Berlin
+49 30 616 71455
info.de@durgopak.com

The patented Carton offers an intelligent solution to the storage of patient information leaflets (PIL)

- Allows for easy storage of acompact leaflet
- Offers maximum room for a range of pharma products
- Reduces overall size of outer packaging
- Supports patient compliance
- Streamline your manufacturing processes
- Reduce poor product insertion
- Integrates into your current production line
- Conveniently connected to the outer carton
- Both for ethical perspective or an OTC drug

PHARMA PACKAGING INNOVATIONS

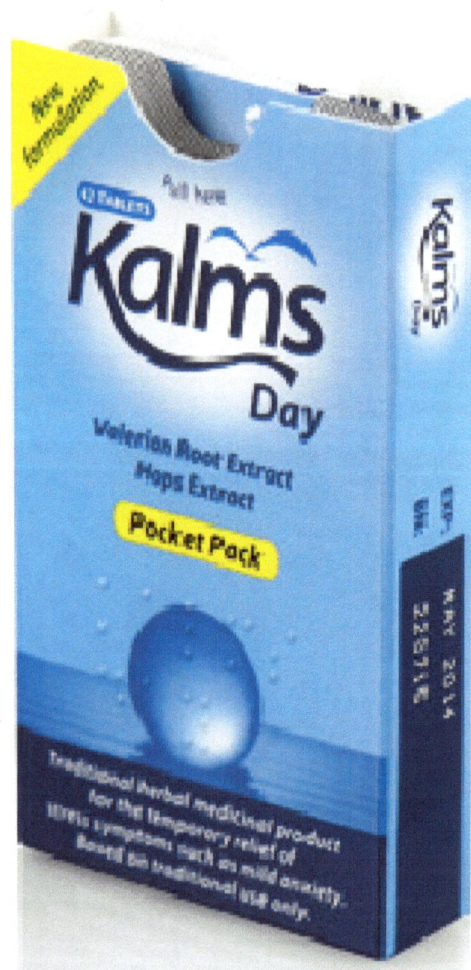

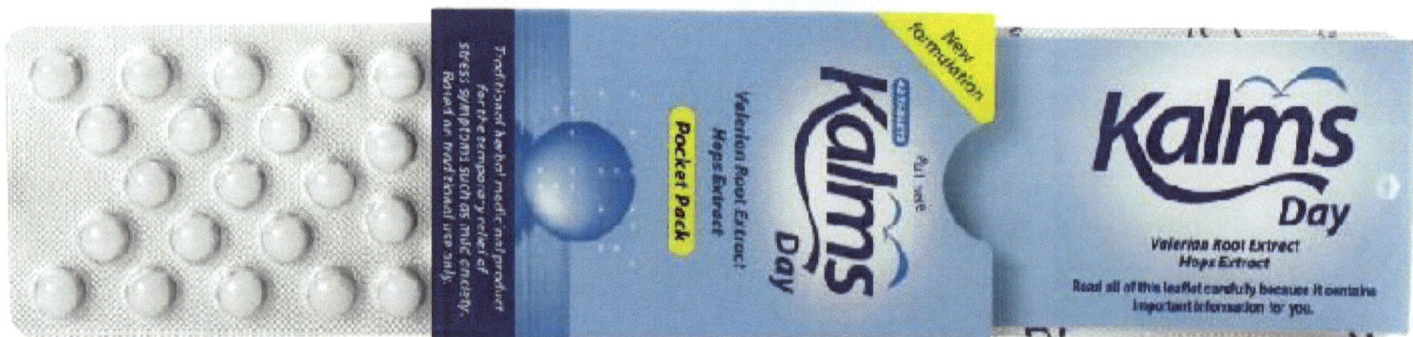

PHARMA PACKAGING INNOVATIONS

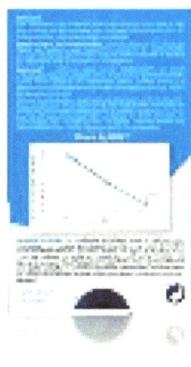

Manufacturer/Designer

Burgopak Germany Ltd.
Alexandrinenstraße 2-3 Aufgang C
10969 Berlin
+49 30 616 71455
info.de@burgopak.com

The slider design adds value for brand owners.

Unique printable areas on the pack offer maximum opportunity for brand communication.

The sliding mechanism supplies a competitive point of differentiation, encouraging consumers to engage with the product through the interactive opening and closing mechanism.

The compactness of the design also optimizes retail shelf space, while simultaneously reducing shipping costs.

The slider design also provides maximum protection for the blister, reducing the risk of tablets being accidentally released.

Retains the patient information and blisters, while being durable, engaging, and making all components easily accessible.

Highly portable and durable format to the wear and tear during on the go usage

PHARMA PACKAGING INNOVATIONS

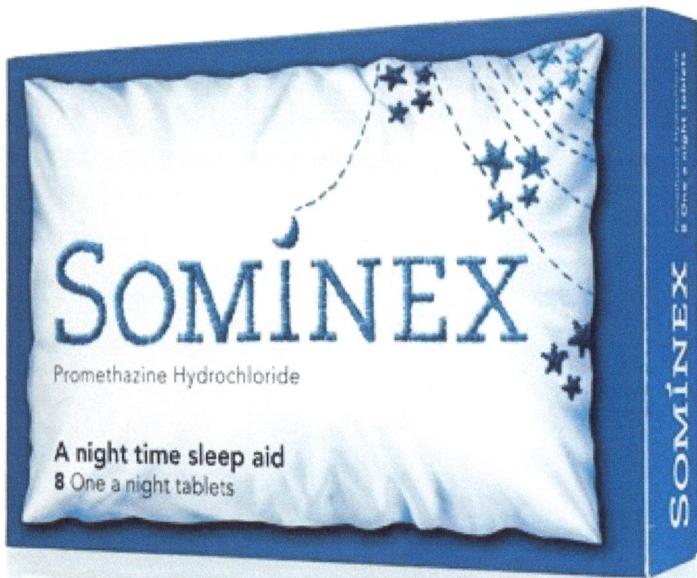

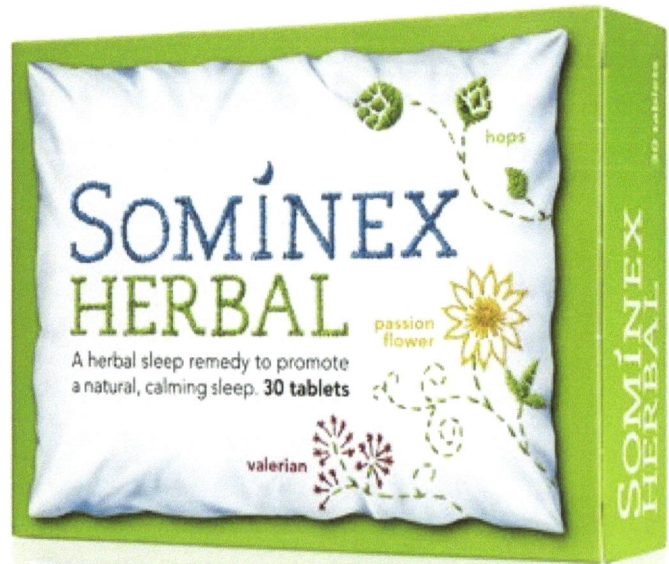

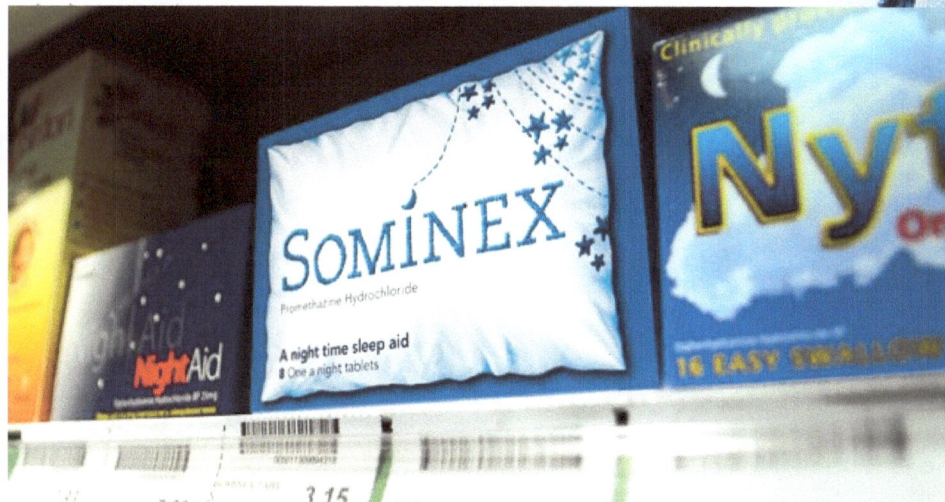

Manufacturer/Designer

Design Bridge London18
Clerkenwell Close
LondonEC1R 0QN
United Kingdom
T: +44 (0)20 7814 9922
F: +44 (0)20 7814 9024
sales_london@designbridge.com

Sominex is a powerful and effective OTC sleep remedy.

The brand was hindered by low awareness and a dark, serious image that appealed mainly to long-term insomniacs and fuelled other consumers' fears and perceptions about the implications of sleeplessness and taking addictive 'sleeping pills'.

Sleep-deprived people who are unwilling to identify themselves as having a 'serious' problem or, worse, a edical condition.

Adopted a more category challenging solution, breaking through the psychological barriers with pure emotion.

Design reassures with soothing images of soft, comfortable pillows and bed linen and adds friendly

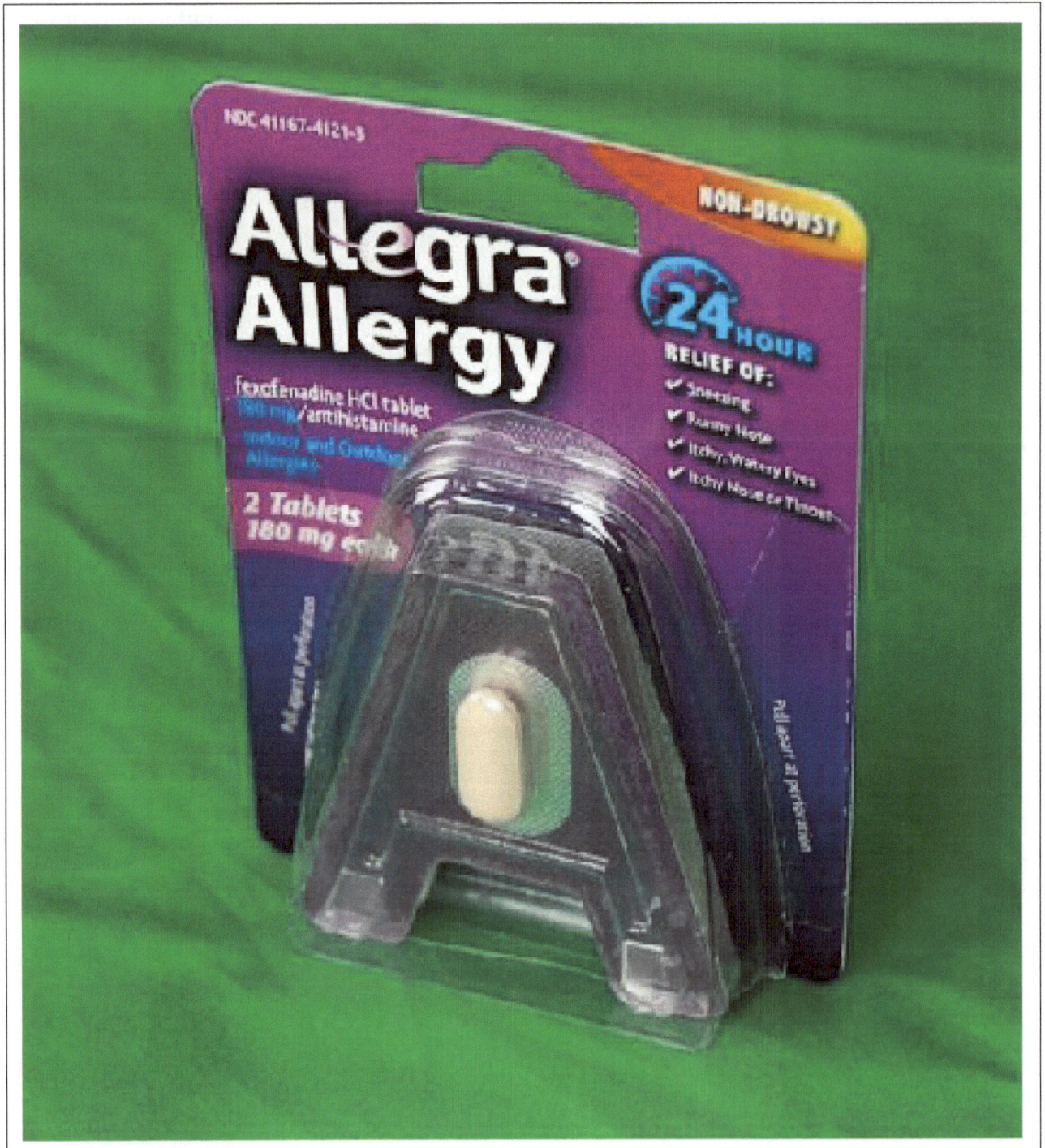

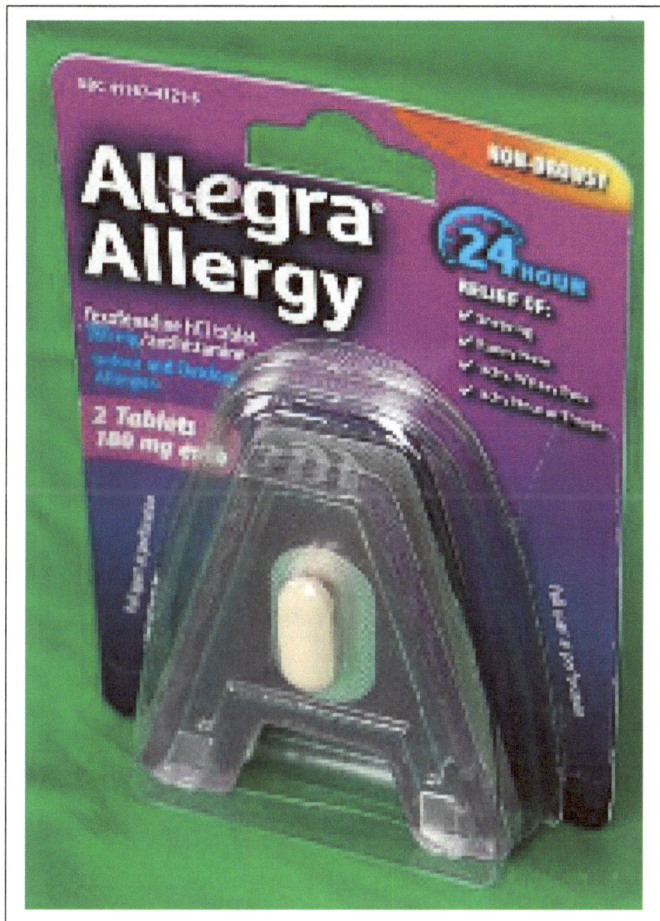

Manufacturer/Designer

**Sanofi US's Chattem
consumer healthcare
division**

The primary packaging is distinctive, particularly in that it is patterned after the Allegra "A" logo.

The pack is easy to carry, simple to open The blister is made in non square, non rectangle shape

Trays made from paperboard certified by the Sustainable Forestry Initiative, and lightweight blister foil material.

This initiative was taken to launch a trial pack for allergy tablets that can be sold as OTC

The clamshell is made of RPET that houses the two A-shaped samples

PHARMA PACKAGING INNOVATIONS

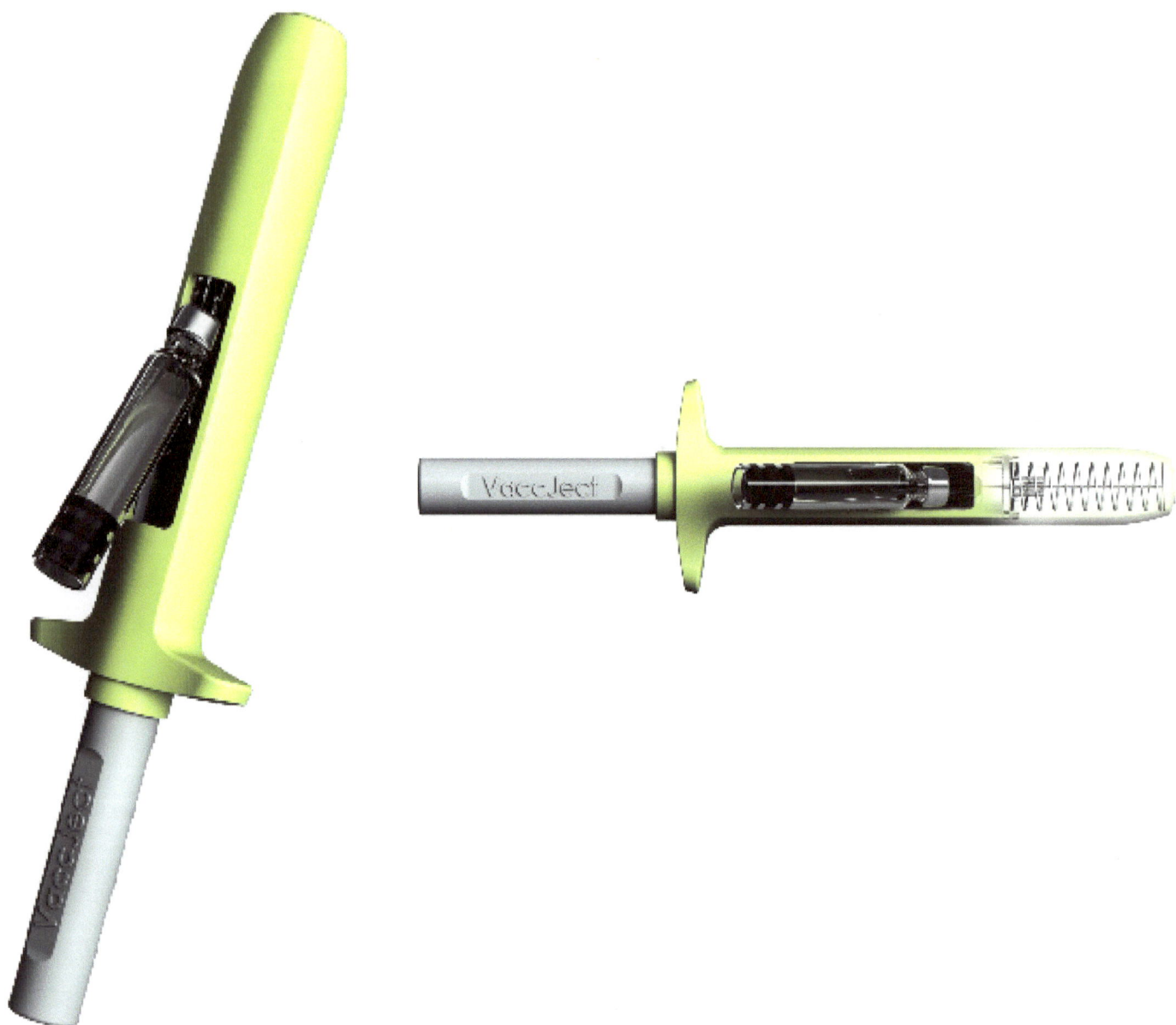

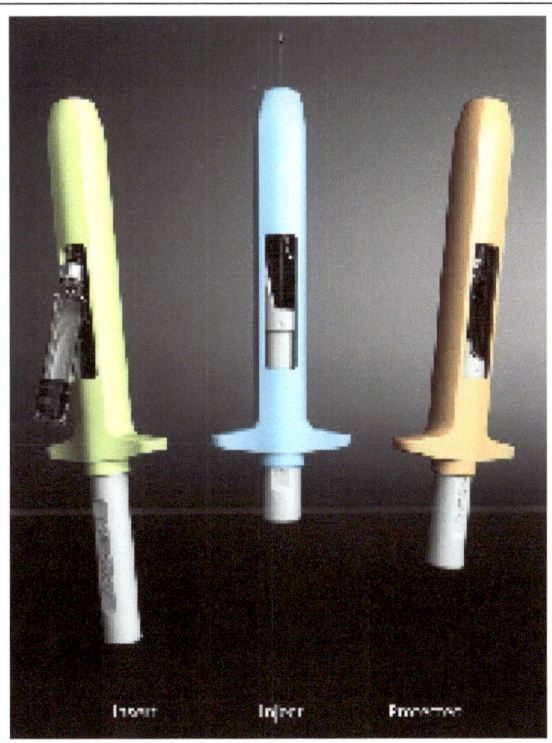

Insert   Inject   Protected

Manufacturer/Designer

DUOJECT MEDICAL SYSTEMS INC.
50 CHEMIN DE GASPÉ, COMPLEX B-5
BROMONT (QUEBEC) CANADA
J2L 2N8
T: 877-534-3666
F: 450-534-3700
Email: E-NOVATIONS@DUOJECT.COM

Drug separate from device - minimize cold chain storage and transportation

Cartridge based alternative to pre-filled syringes

Built-in needlestick protection – no secondary operation required

No exposed needle before or after device use and activation

Dry needle system eliminates potential drug needle / adhesive interaction

Various needle gauges and lengths available

Unique design ensures product differentiation

Child Resistant Dispensing Pack

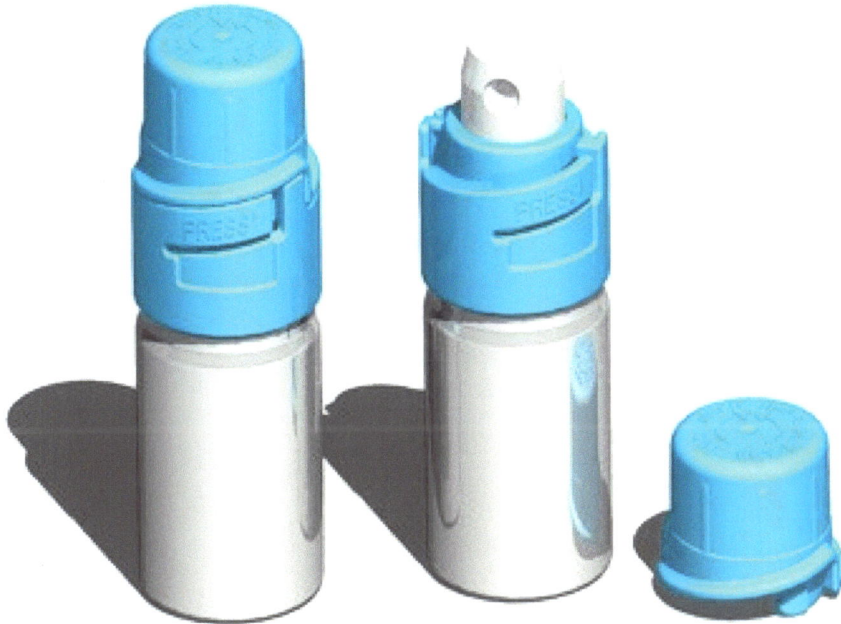

Manufacturer/Designer

Nolato Jaycare
(Portsmouth)
Walton Road
Farlington
Portsmouth.
PO6 1TS United Kingdom
Tel. : +44 (0)2392 370 102
Fax. : +44 (0)2392 380 314
Email: info@nolato.com
website: www.nolato.com

- Child Resistant Dispensing Pack for an anaesthetic spray

- The opening procedures are based on a squeeze and turn principal.

- However, unlike traditional CR closures where the cap is squeezed, the operation has been transferred to the collar component.

- This adds to the security and also minimises the risk of children using their teeth to open the pack.

- The closure system is intentionally allowed to rotate on the container in order to help prevent the product from being forced open.

- Instead of a thread-form, the closure utilises a bayonet type fit to simplify the re-closure operation.

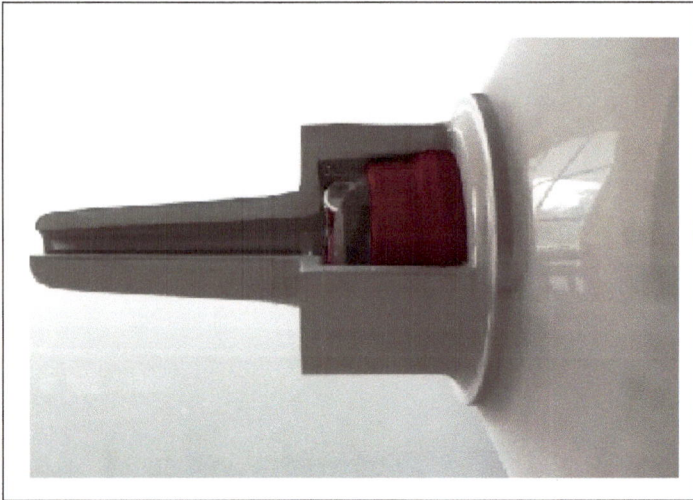

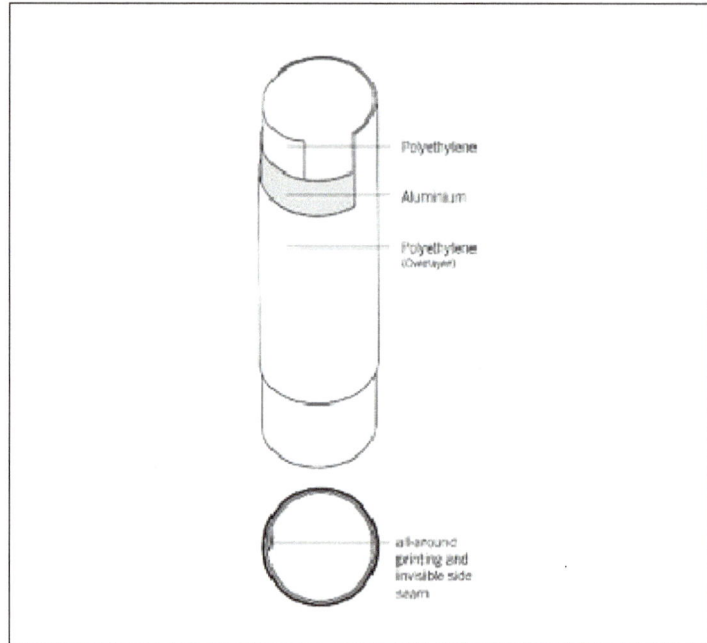

Polyethylene

Aluminium

Polyethylene
(Overlayer)

all-around
printing and
invisible side
seam

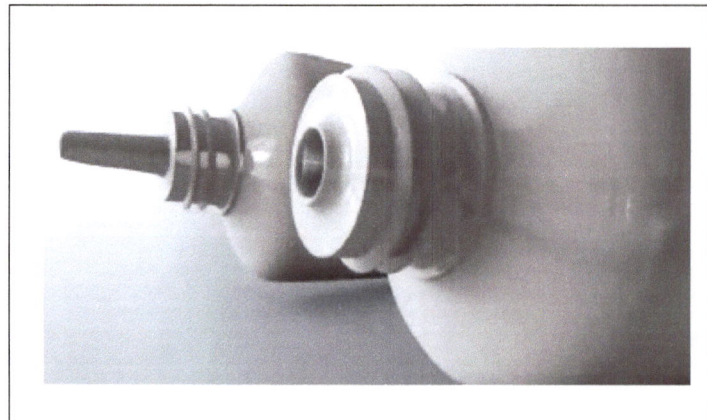

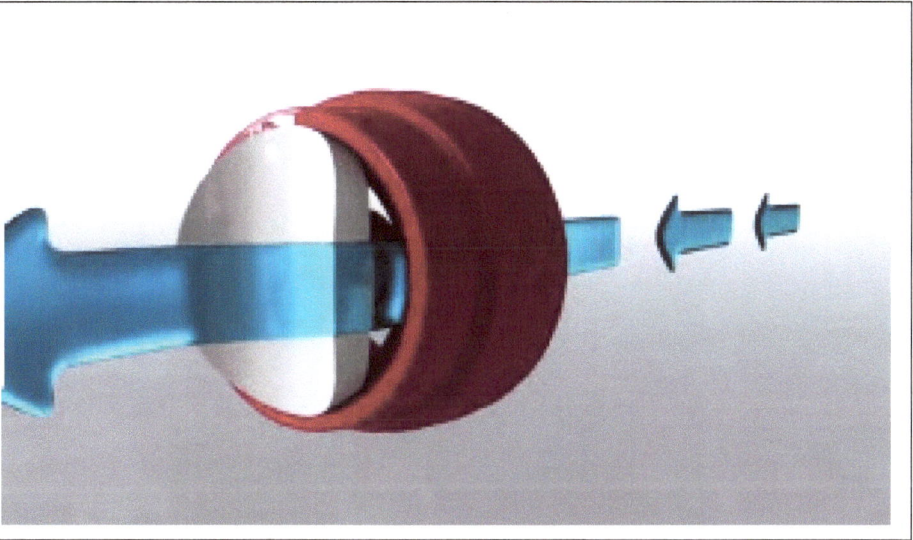

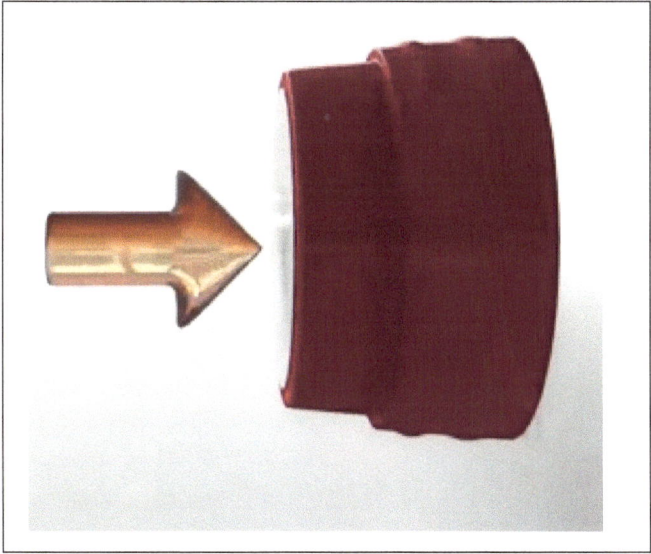

Manufacturer/Designer

Hoffmann Neopac AG
Burgdorfstrasse 22
Postfach
3672 Oberdiessbach
Switzerland
T: +41 (0)31 770 11 11
F: +41 (0)31 770 13 13
info(at)neopac.com

The cosmetic, pharma industries places ever more demanding requirements on packaging

First there is the need to protect increasingly sensitive contents and second packaging must meet the aesthetic standards of the market.

The development of the new AirShield™ Tube fulfil these requirements with one tube.

This is a two-component valve that prevents air from flowing back into the tube when the contents are dispensed.

The combination of the barrier properties of Polyfoil® and AirShield™ is perfectly suited to give maximum protection to oxygen sensitive products, even after the tube is first opened.

This ensures that the quality and effect of the products remain throughout their use.

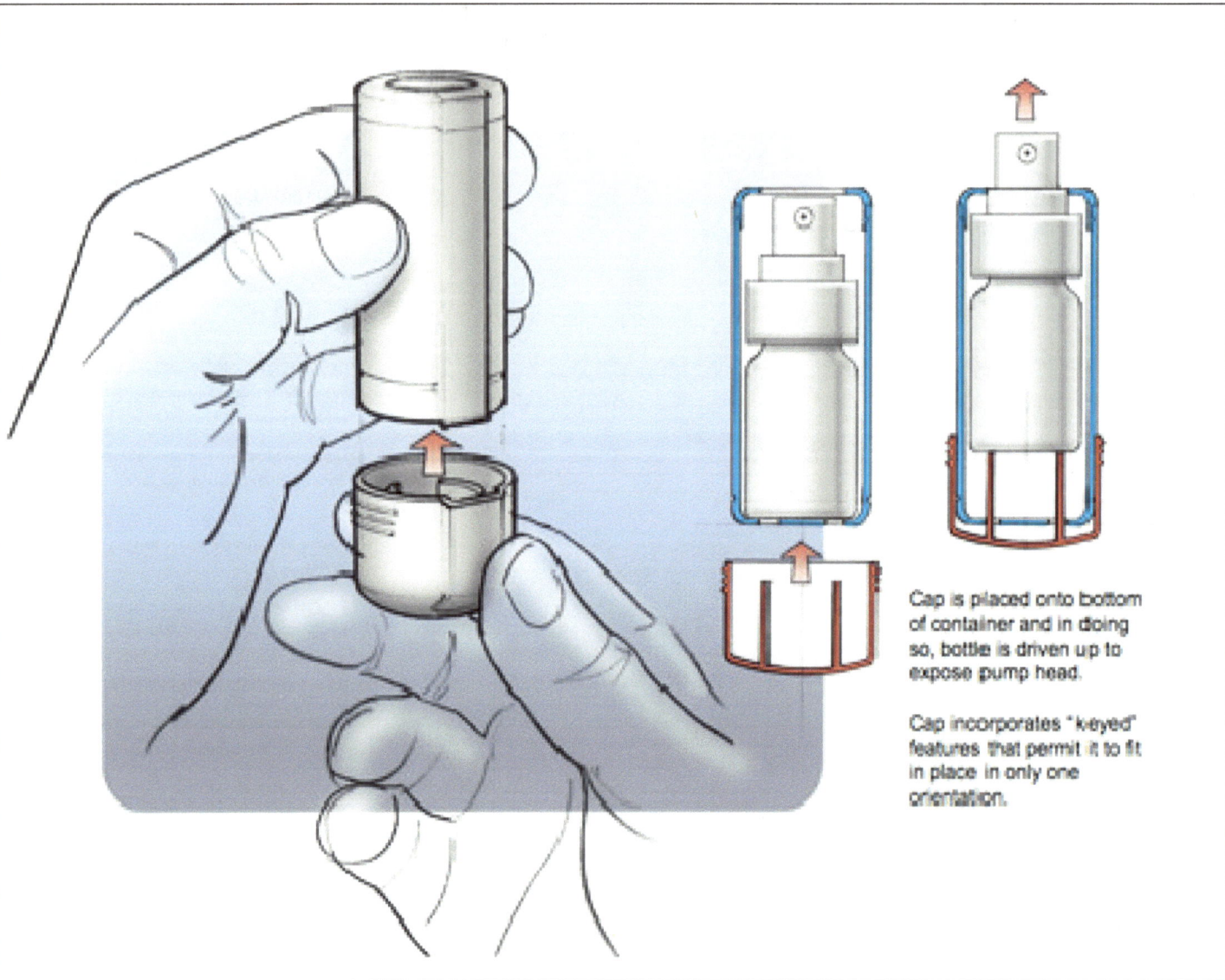

Cap is placed onto bottom of container and in doing so, bottle is driven up to expose pump head.

Cap incorporates "keyed" features that permit it to fit in place in only one orientation.

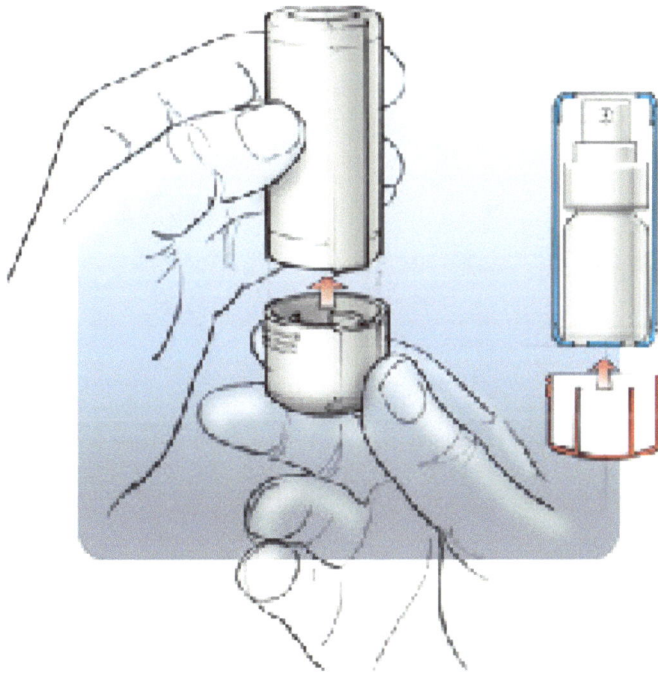

Cap is placed onto bottom
of container and in doing
so bottle is driven so to
expose pump head.

Cap incorporates "keyed"
features that permit it to fit
in place in only one
orientation.

Manufacturer/Designer

DeJonge Associates, Inc.
Stuart DeJonge, Principal
804 Heron Point Circle
DeLand, FL 32724
SDeJonge@PharmaPackagingDesign.com
386-228-1004

To dispense a product using this child-resistant overcap, the consumer removes the cap, inverts it, and slides it on to the bottom of the container where it snaps into place.

This action pushes the inner pump or aerosol sprayer upward, allowing the consumer to dispense the product. After use, the cap is removed from the bottom
of the outer container, the spray unit drops down inside, and the cap is placed back on top.

This cap design can be utilized with pump or aerosol sprayers and is ideal for smaller, easily carried containers.

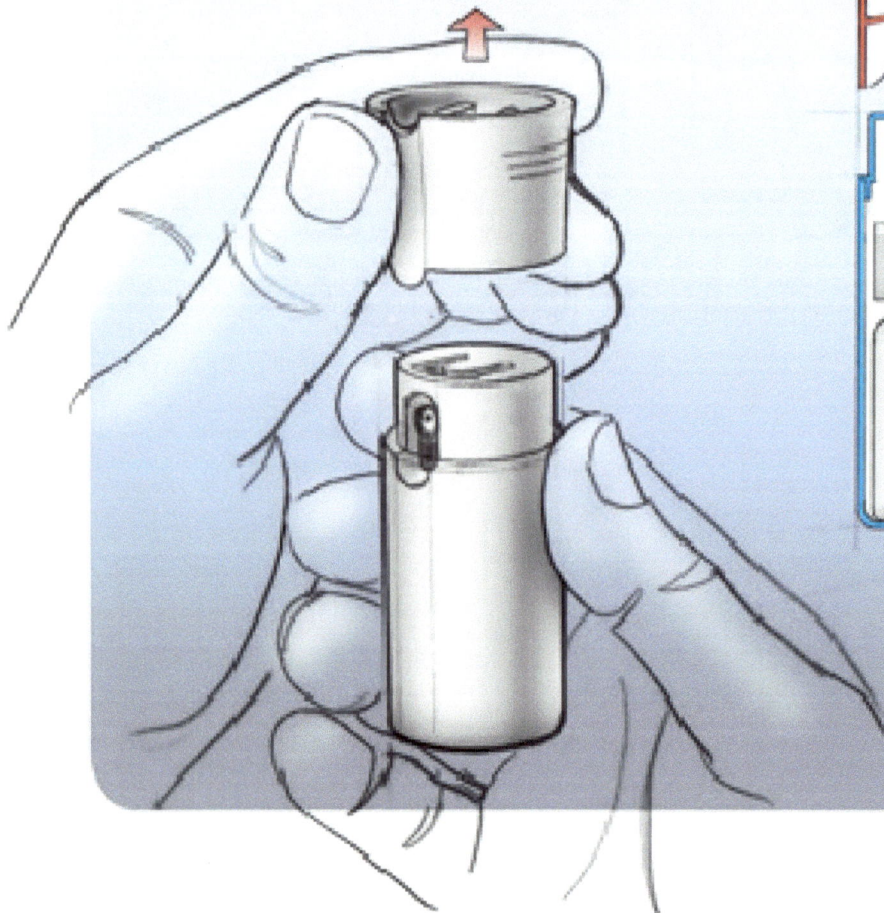

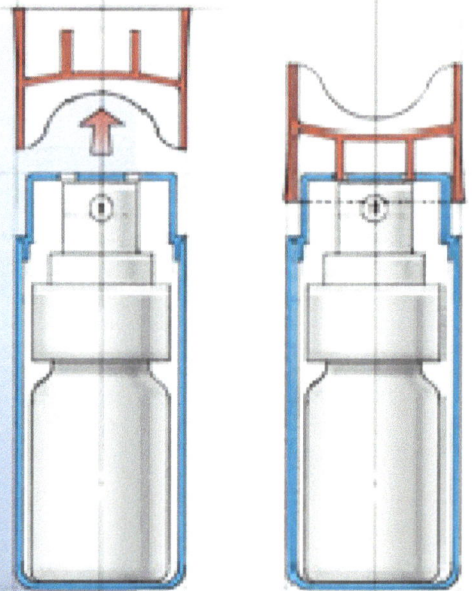

Flip / Flap cap is lifted off, flipped over, then repositioned on top of container.

-Tip / Hood cap is lifted off, flipped over, then repositioned on top of container.

Manufacturer/Designer

DeJonge Associates, Inc.
Stuart DeJonge, Principal
804 Heron Point Circle
DeLand, FL 32724
SDeJonge@PharmaPackagingDesign.com
386-228-1004

In this variant, the consumer removes the cap, inverts it, and slides it back on top of the container.

Downward pressure applied to the inverted cap now pushes on the inner sprayer and dispenses the product

After use, the cap is removed from the top of the outer container, flipped over and placed back on top of the container.

This cap design can be utilized with pump or aerosol sprayers and is ideal for smaller, easily carried

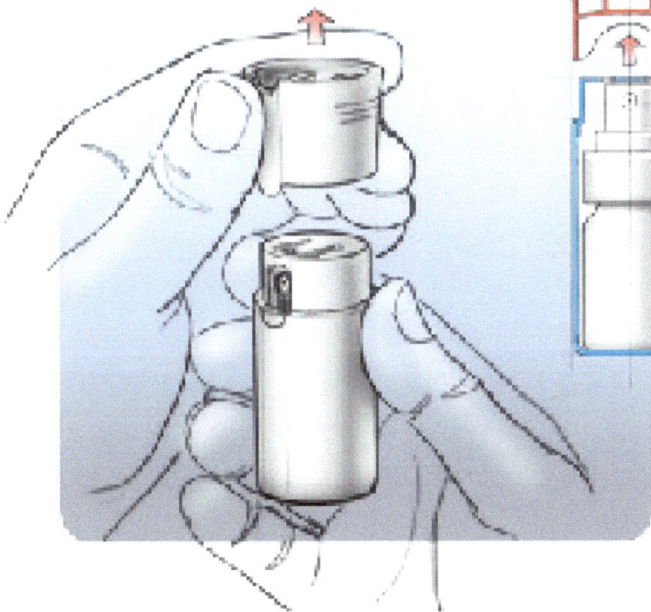

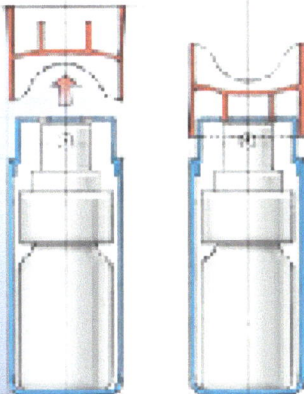

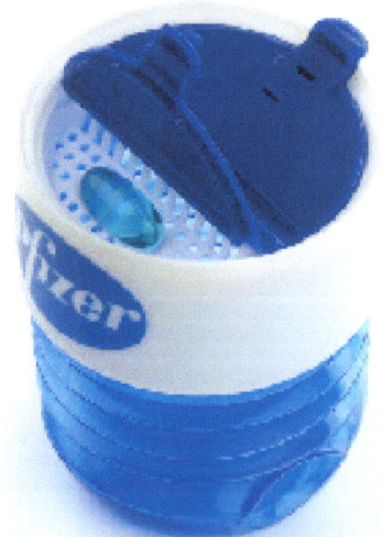

PHARMA PACKAGING INNOVATIONS

Manufacturer/Designer

Anatomed, Inc.
1000 Lake St., Bldg D
Ramsey, NJ 07446
p: (201) 825-7676
info@reflexhammer.com

Easy access, hermetically sealed pill storage compartment

Patient friendly, proprietary design

Conveniently opens and collapses for storage and travel

Holds 6 ounces of water

Unique receptacle aligns pill and maximizes water flow for swallowing

Dishwasher safe (top shelf)

Large imprint areas for branding,co-branding, and product info

Ideal pharma rep handout to physicians, or part of patient care/sample kit

PHARMA PACKAGING INNOVATIONS

Auto Drop & Auto Squeeze

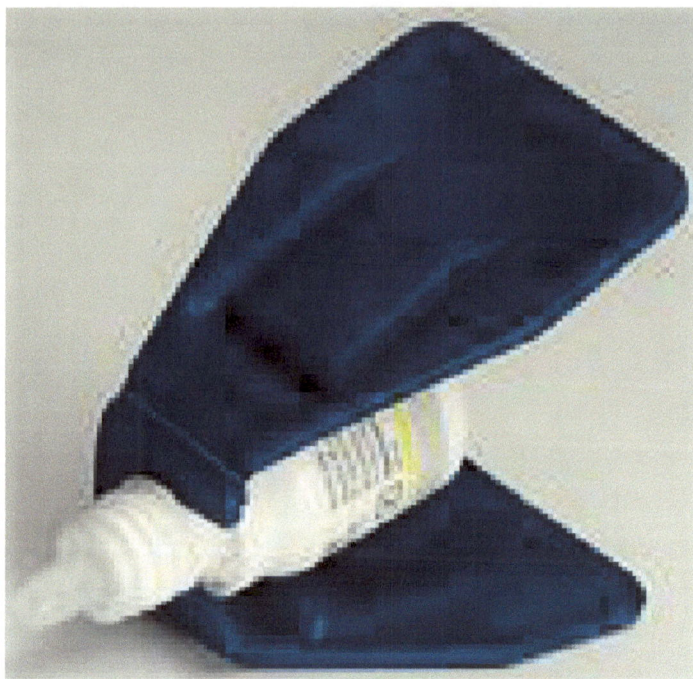

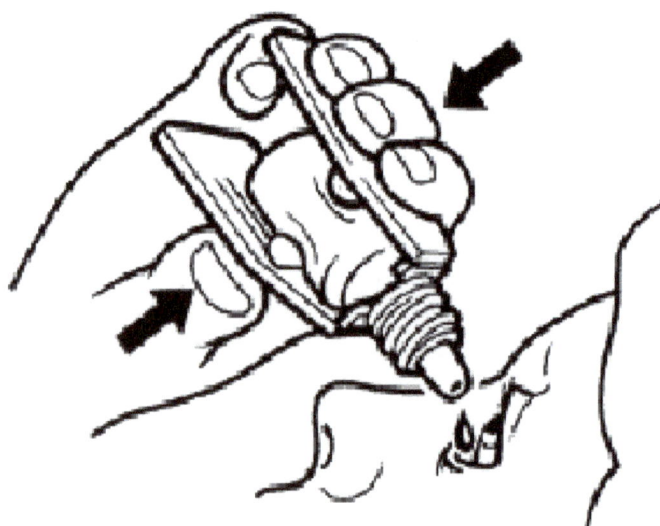

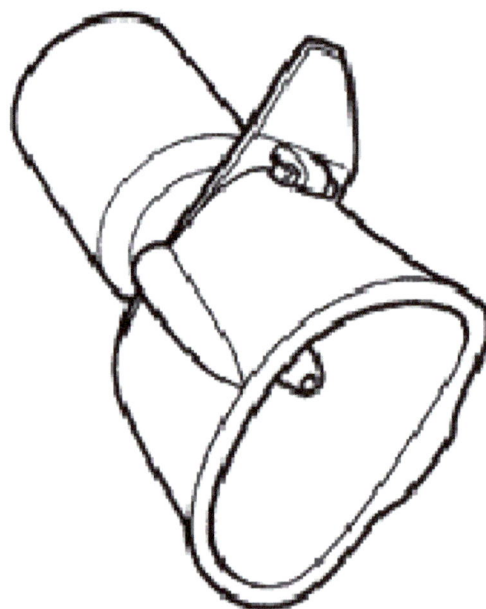

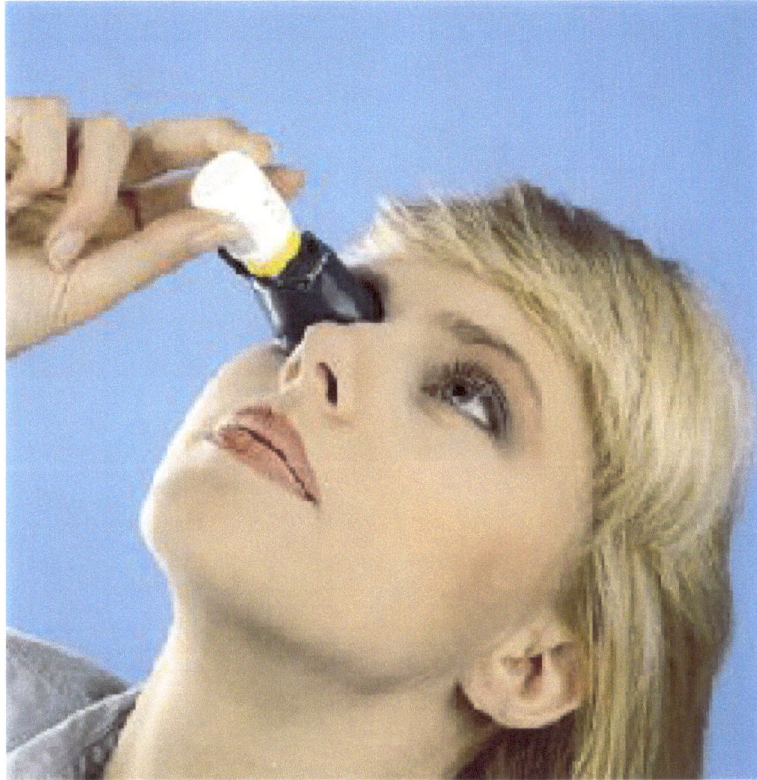

Manufacturer/Designer

Owmen Mumford Ltd
Brook Hill
Woodstock
Oxford
OX20 1TU
United Kingdom
T.01993 812021
F.01993 813466
E.info@owenmumford.co.uk

Autodrop device clips onto the majority of eyedrop bottles and holds the bottle at the correct angle over the eye

A small lip holds the lower eyelid open to prevent blinking while a unique pinhole directs the eyesight upward,away from descending drops Medication goes in the eye, not down the cheek

Autosqueeze instillation aids are designed for patients who require ophthalmic preparations but have difficulty taking them.

The device helps patients with weak or arthritic fingers easily grasp and dispense ophthalmic medication.

Simply clip the dropping bottle into the device and

Infant formula tub with AccuMeasure scoop

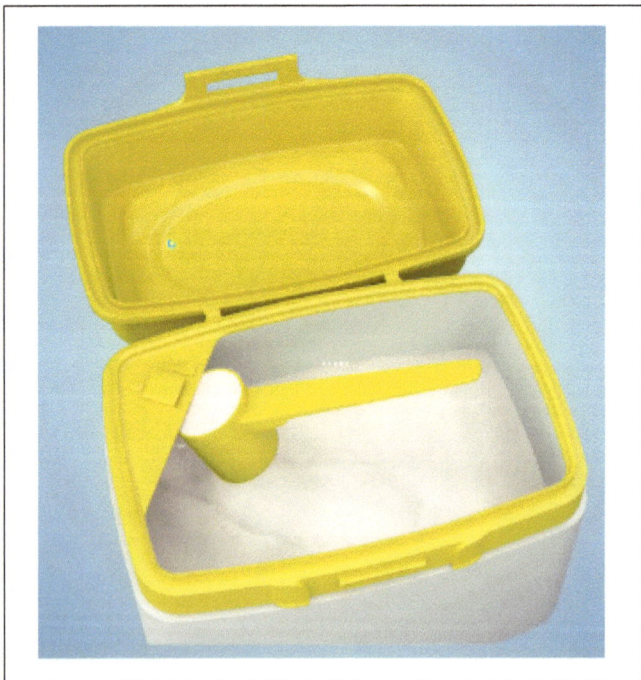

Manufacturer/Designer

Perrigo Nutritionals
Corporate Information
Perrigo Company Corporate
Office
515 Eastern Avenue
Allegan, Michigan 49010
T: (269) 673-8451
E:PediatricComments@perrigo.com

An AccuMeasure™ scoop leveler for more accurate feedings

CleanPull™ technology that easily removes a foil liner with one pull

SimpleSlide™ scoop storage for less mess

A longer scoop handle for hygienic scooping

A 100% leak detection system that improves quality and freshness

Anti-theft tag compatibility that protects the product where it is sold in retail stores

The white base tub is blow-molded of a multilayer HDPE that includes an ethylene vinyl alcohol barrier

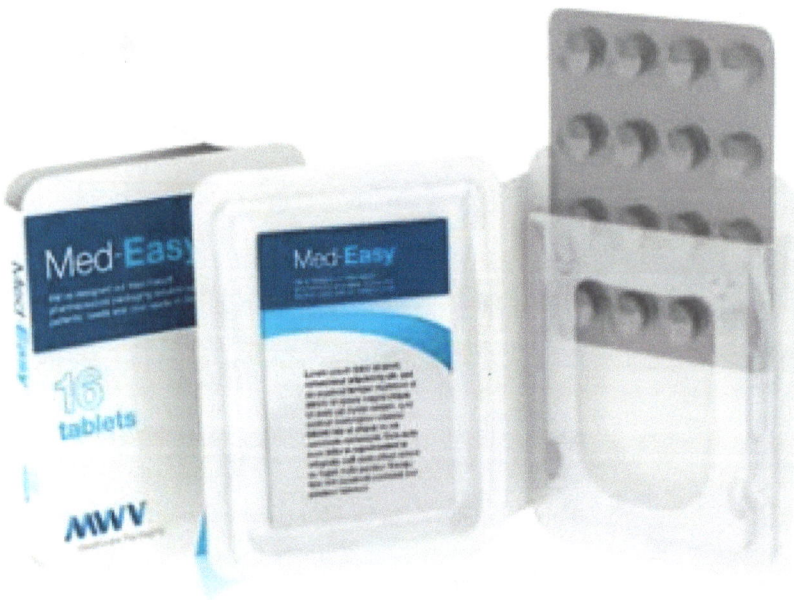

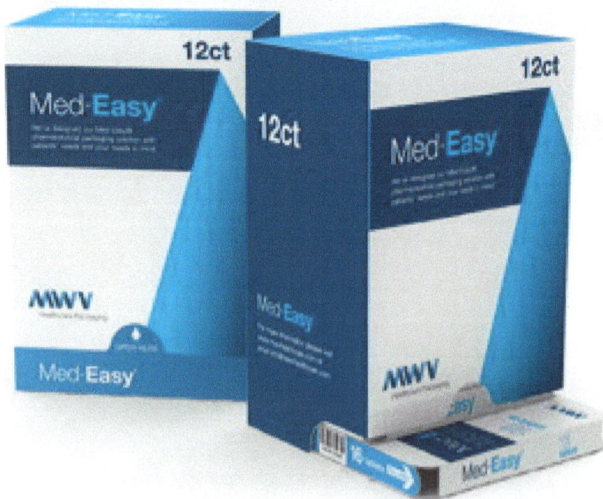

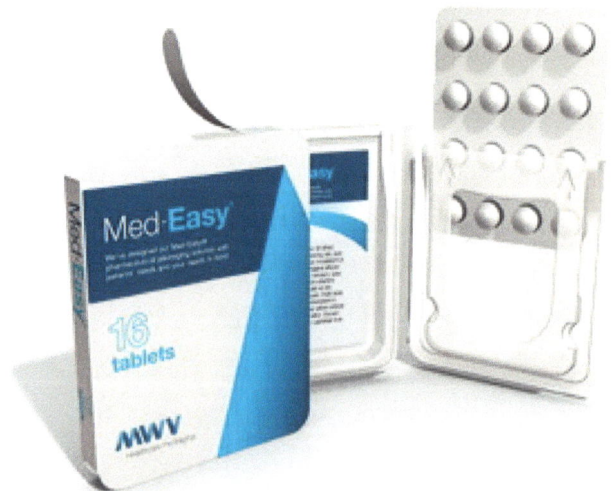

PHARMA PACKAGING INNOVATIONS

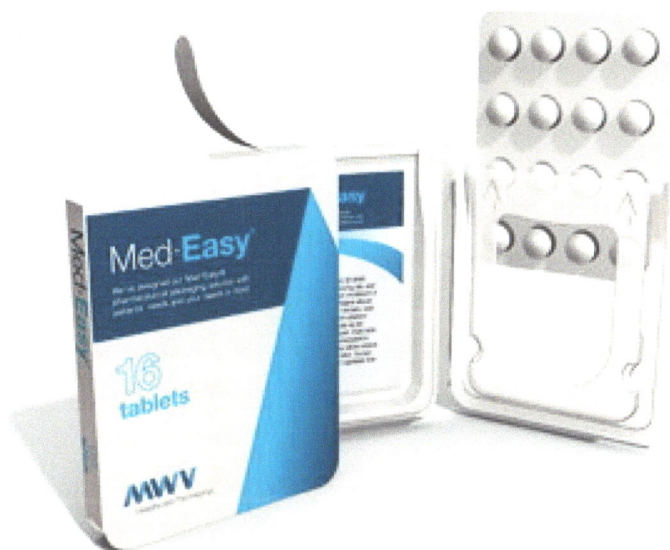

Manufacturer/Designer

Med Easy
+44 7917 838491
healthcare@mwv.com
mwvhealthcare.com

Portable that can even fit inside shirt pocket

One handed, simple to useoperation by slider blister while dispensing

Unique design that differentiate it from other pharma packs

Also the outer carton provides extra space for branding and labeling

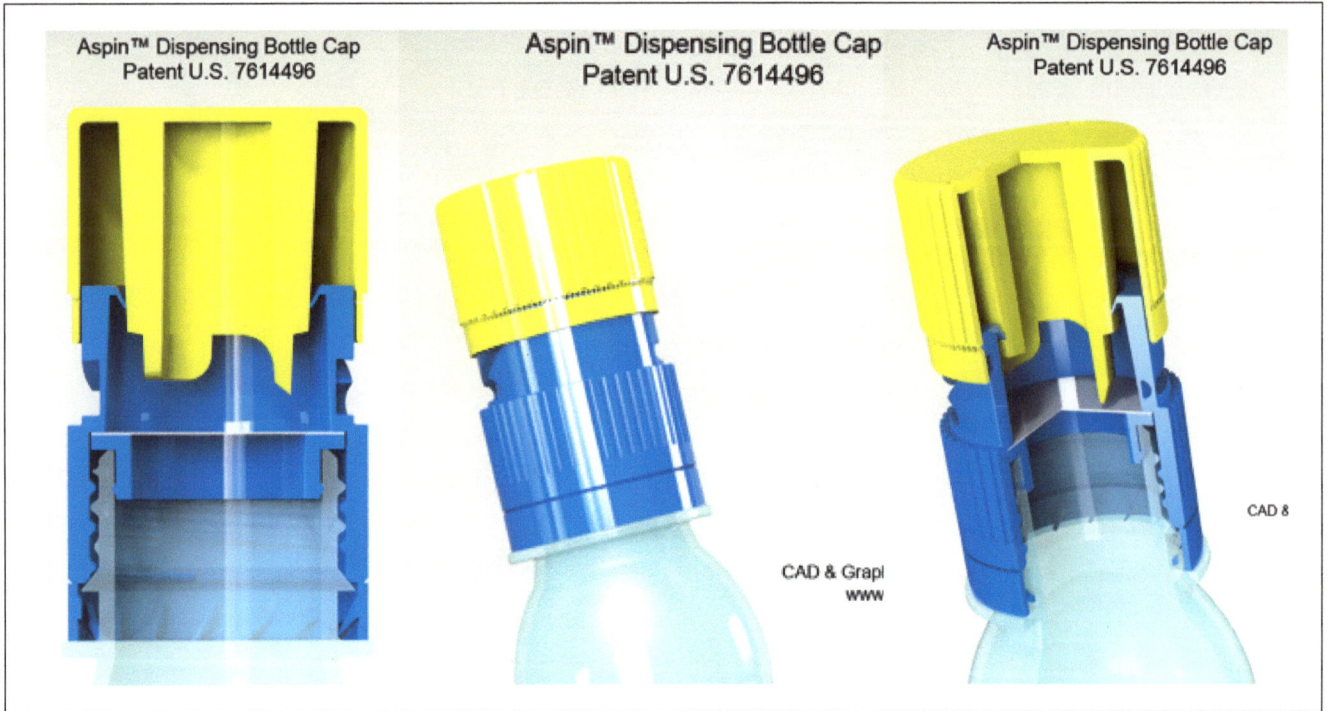

Aspin™ Dispensing Bottle Cap
Patent U.S. 7614496

Aspin™ Dispensing Bottle Cap
Patent U.S. 7614496

Aspin™ Dispensing Bottle Cap
Patent U.S. 7614496

CAD & Graph
www

CAD 8

Aspin™ Dispensing Bottle Cap
Patent U.S. 7614496

CAD & Graph
www.

Manufacturer/Designer

Med Easy
+44 7917 838491
healthcare@mwv.com
mwvhealthcare.com

For dry drugs form prior to usage with activation in aqueous form.

Easier for on the go use

This is a kind of dispenser caps, designed for Aspirin wherein the additive is retained in an isolated condition within a sealed chamber inside the bottle cap, but in fluid communication with the liquid, such as water, within the bottle.

The Aspin cap has a downward extending protrusion to breech the seal of the chamber, thereby releasing the additive retained within the bottle cap, which than mixes with the water

Pharmaceutical

Break Through

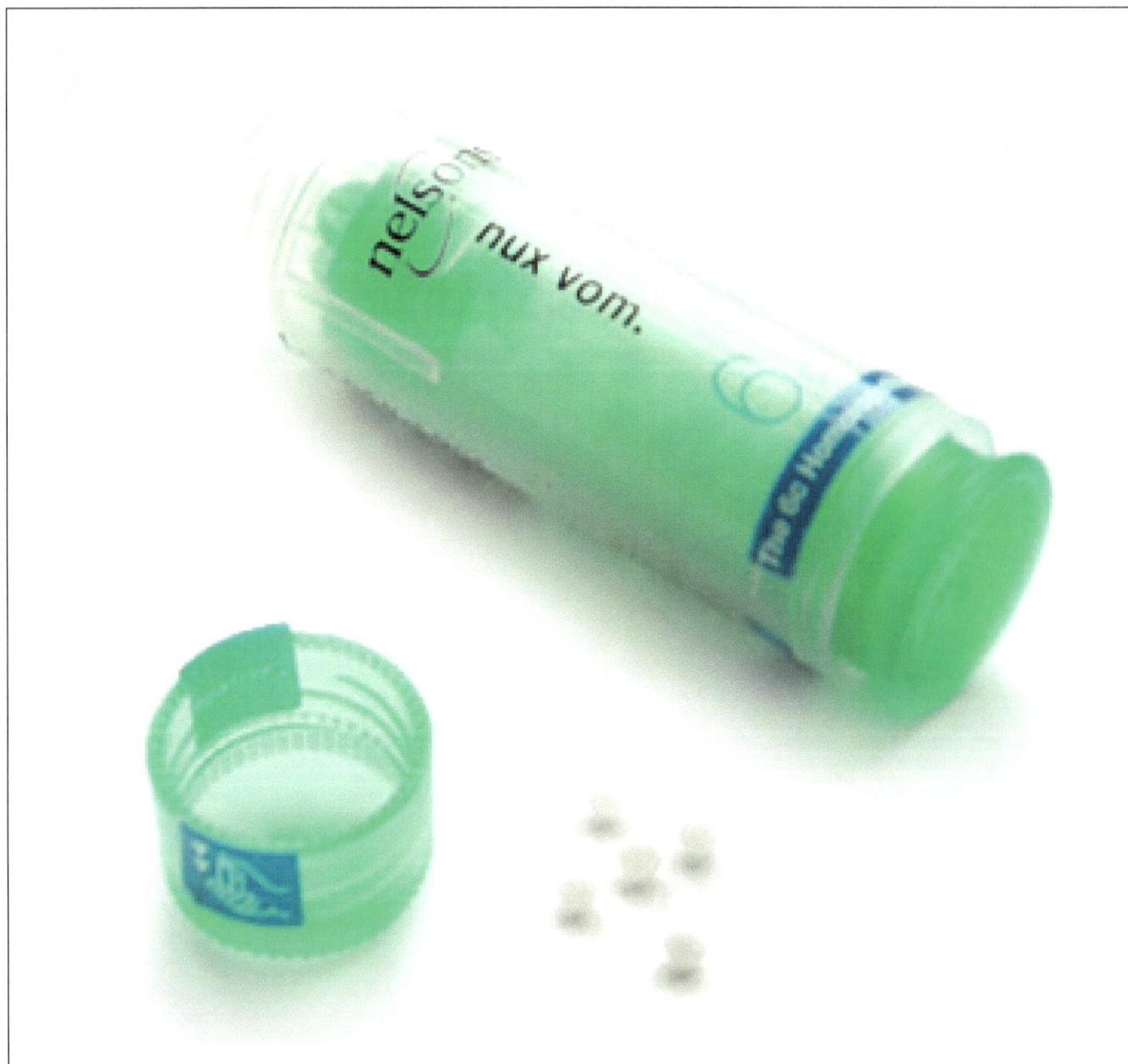

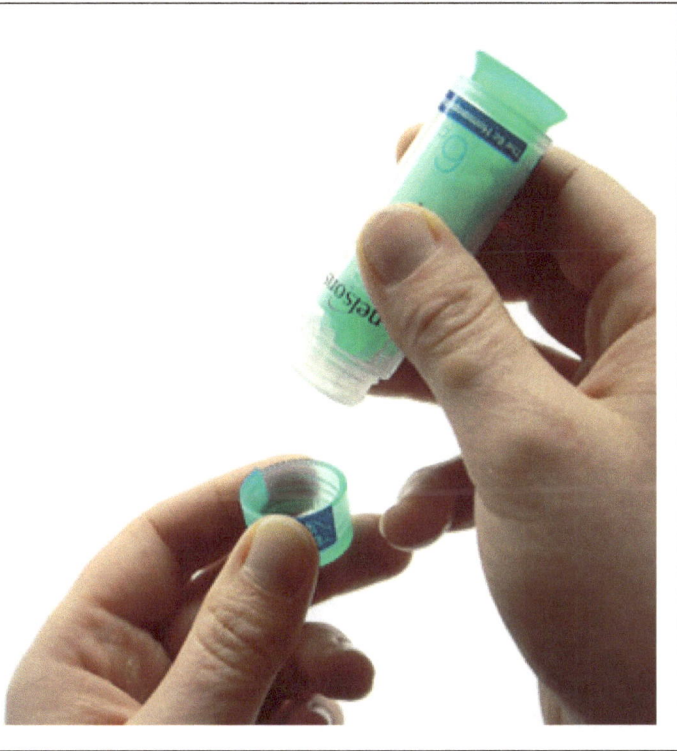

Manufacturer/Designer

A Nelsons and Co Ltd,
Nelsons House, 83 Parkside,
Wimbledon, London SW19 5LP.
Nelsones Homeopathy,
T: +44 (0)20 8780 4200
F: +44 (0)20 8789 0141
E: enquiries@nelsons.net

Homoeopathic pill dispenser. Pharmaceutical packaging Clikpak

This specific dispenser is designed to be used for Homeopathic medicines

Homeopathic remedies are supposednot be touched by hands

Therefore the new pack had to enable patients to dispense a single pill and put it in their mouths without actually handling it

A pill dispenser that reliably releases one pill with each press of the button. One 'click' means one pill

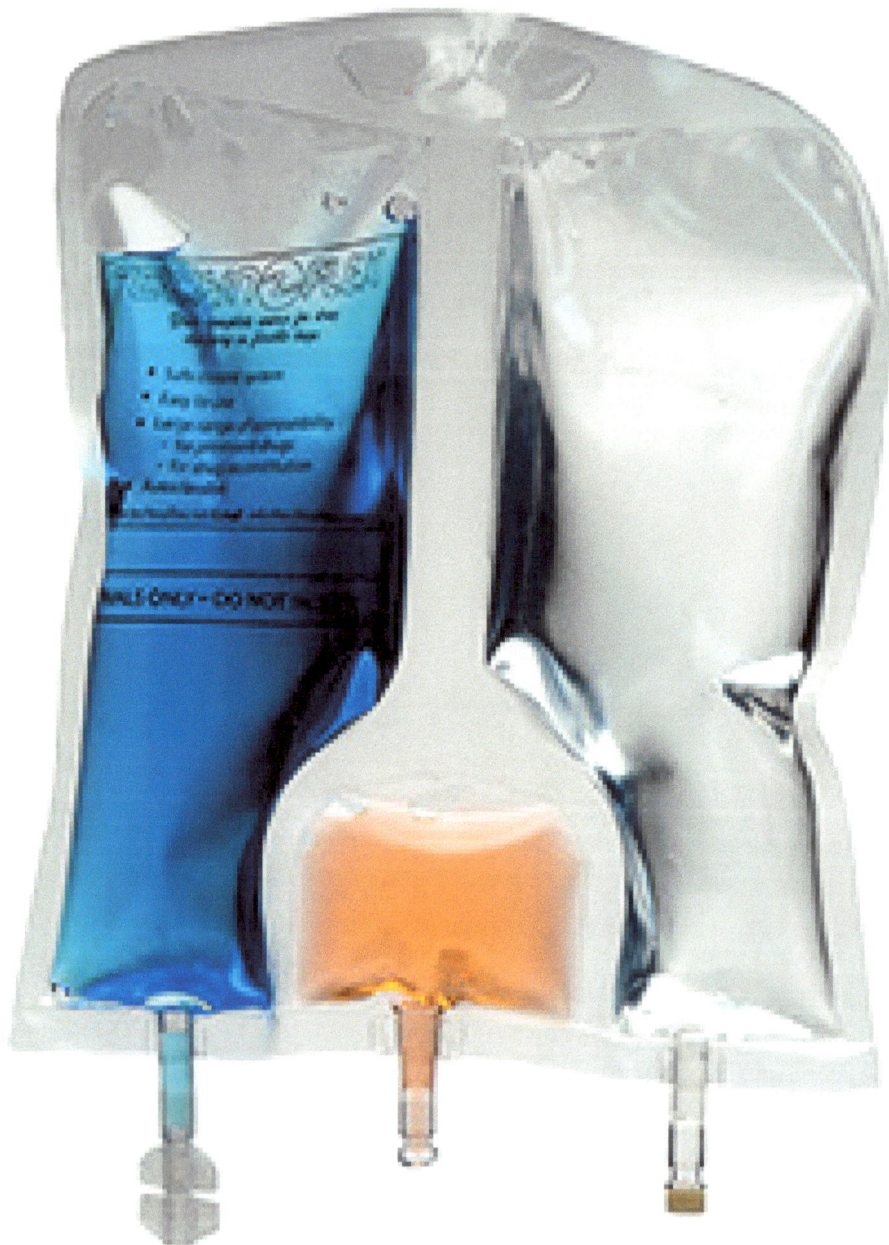

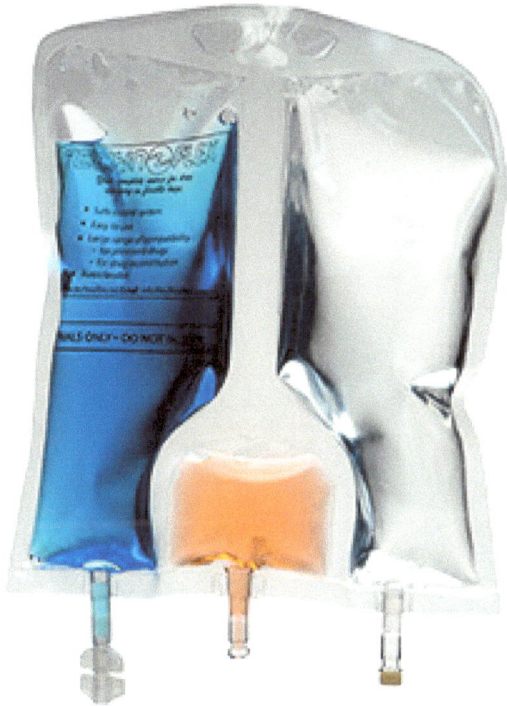

Manufacturer/Designer

Technoflex

Multi-compartment pockets - double, triple or customized can be used for various applications such as parenteral nutrition or drug reconstitution.

These pockets designed to separatedifferent solutions requiring mixture just before administration to the patient.

The separation between the compartments is provided with a separable connector or peel-able seals.

In the latter case, the mixture of solutions is obtained by a simple push of the hand on one of the

PHARMA PACKAGING INNOVATIONS

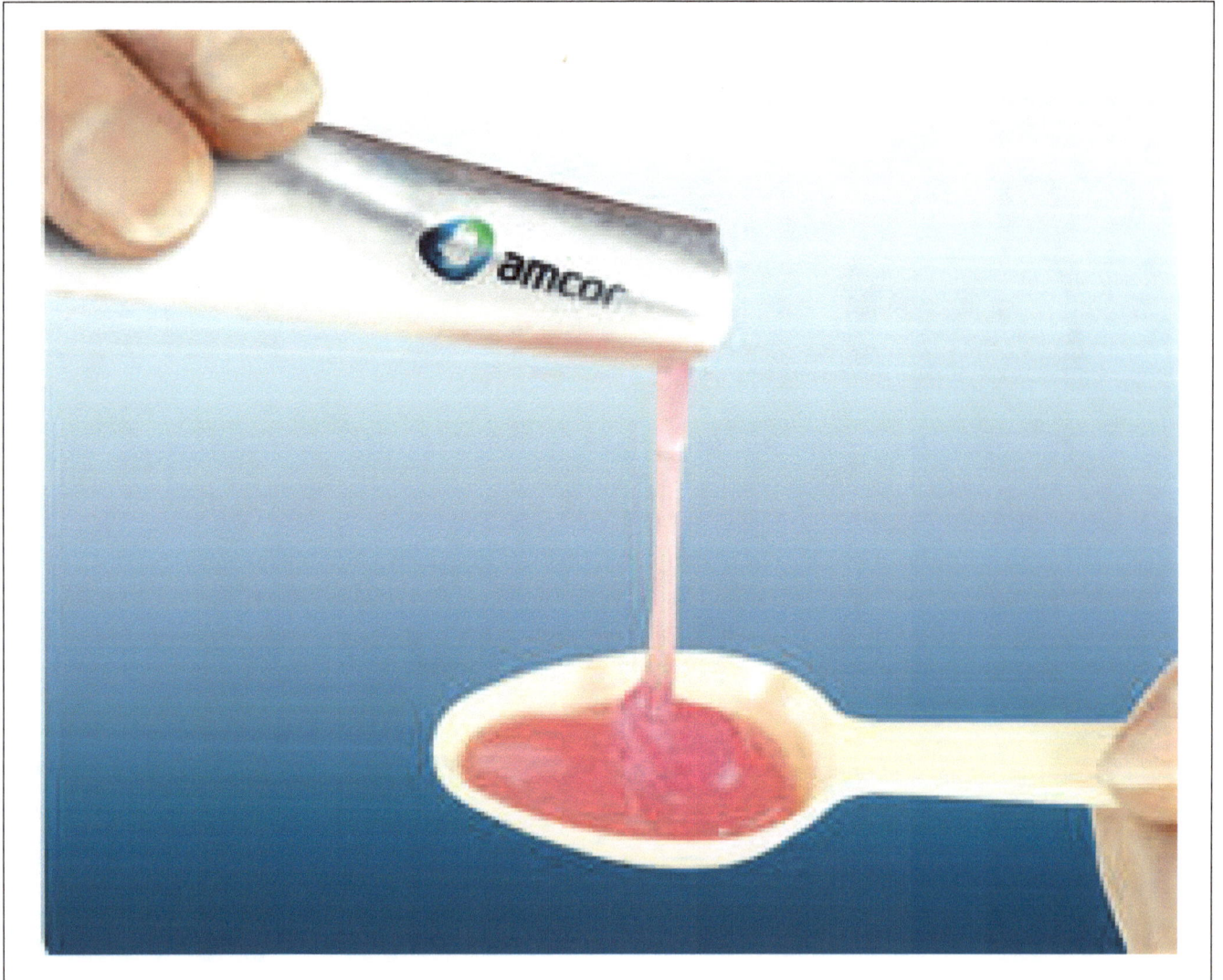

Manufacturer/Designer

Amcor
Medical Packaging Sales
C-519, Sector-19 Noida
Uttar Pradesh 201301 India
Tel: 91 120 2524781
Fax: +91 120 2524067
http://www.amcor.com

Stick packs are a fast growing solution for single-use pharmaceutical applications, providing lightweight, secure and hygienic packaging, perfect for travelling and easy disposal

Good compatibility between the productand package

Excellent seal integrity for highly sensitive or aggressive drugs

Easy to squeeze, convenient andhygienic dispensing

Minimal waste of product and packaging

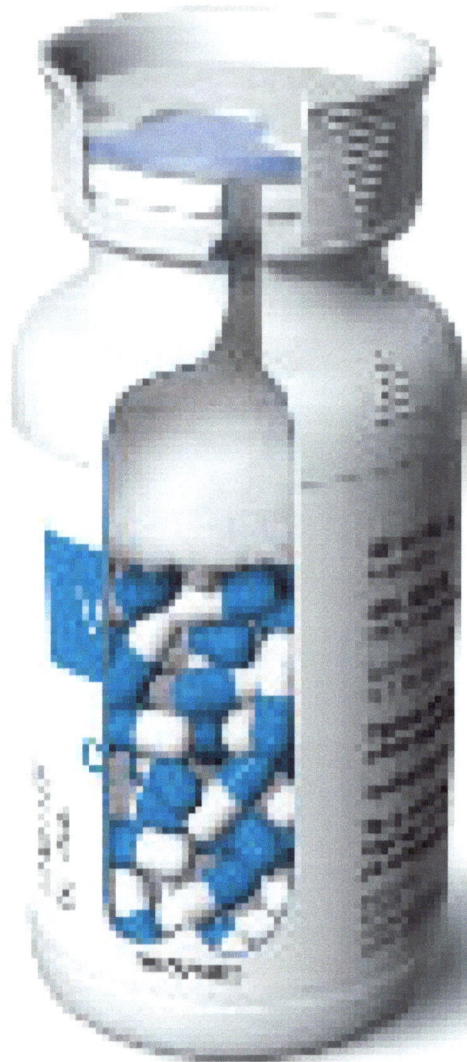

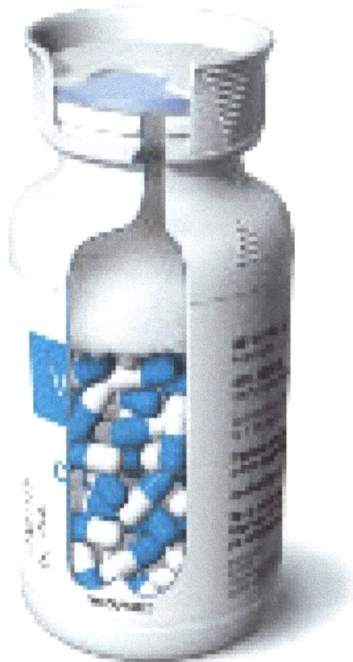

Manufacturer/Designer

Alcan Packaging
8770 W Bryn Mawr Avenue,
Chicago, IL 60631, USA, (773) 399-8000, info.
medflex@alcan.com

Desiccant bottle has desiccant incorporated into the product-contact layer, removing the need for a desiccant sachet inside the bottle.

The bottle offers improved product protectionand longer shelf life while adding line efficiencies that can provide significant production cost savings.

The patent-pending design of this bi-layer, co-extrusion blow molded container

Saves space on the filling line and removes the need for inspection to confirm the presence of desiccant.

Reduces the possibility of product contamination or damage due to desiccant contact.

The Calcium Oxide (CaO) desiccant is blow molded into the bottle's product contact layer

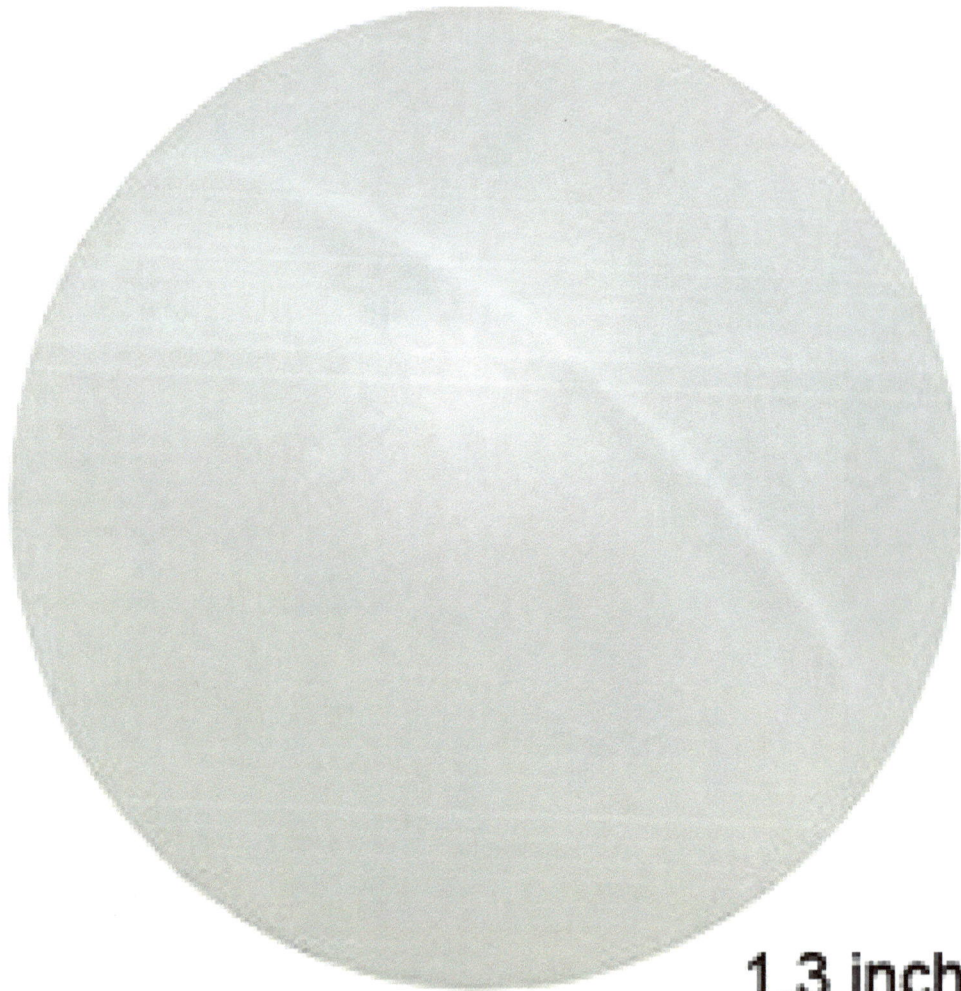

1.3 inch

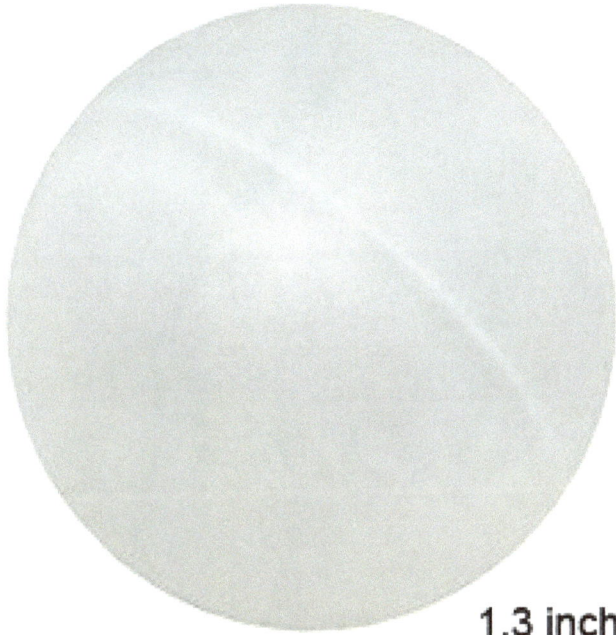

1.3 inch

Manufacturer/Designer

**K K Group and Gerber
Products Company**

They have also designed a new roll-on ball to suit baby powder in 1.4 inch.

Their special design makes it possible to avoid the powder flying effect when applying the baby powder, giving easy use of the product.

And at the same time as applying the product you can give to the baby a comfortable massage thanks of the drawing on the ball.

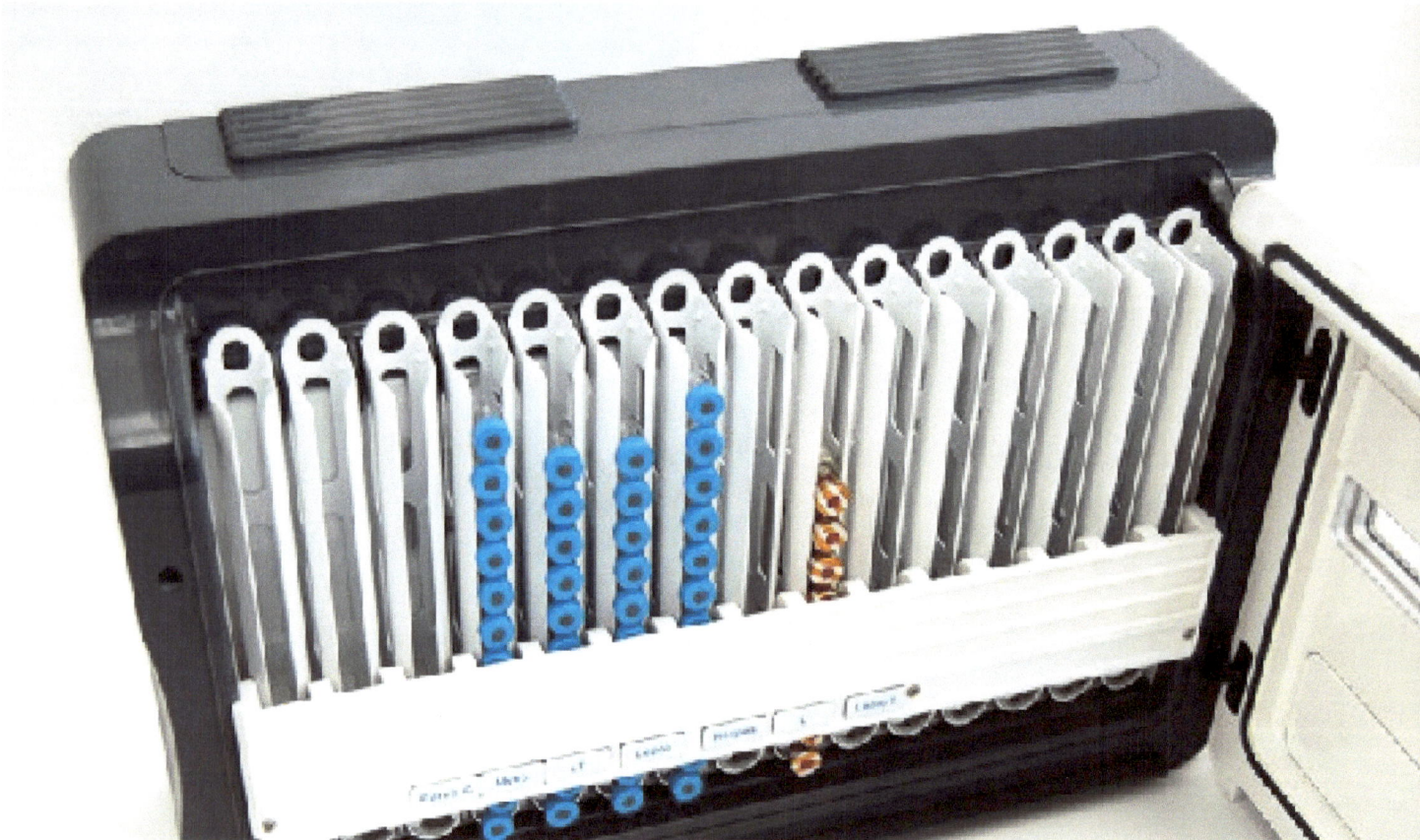

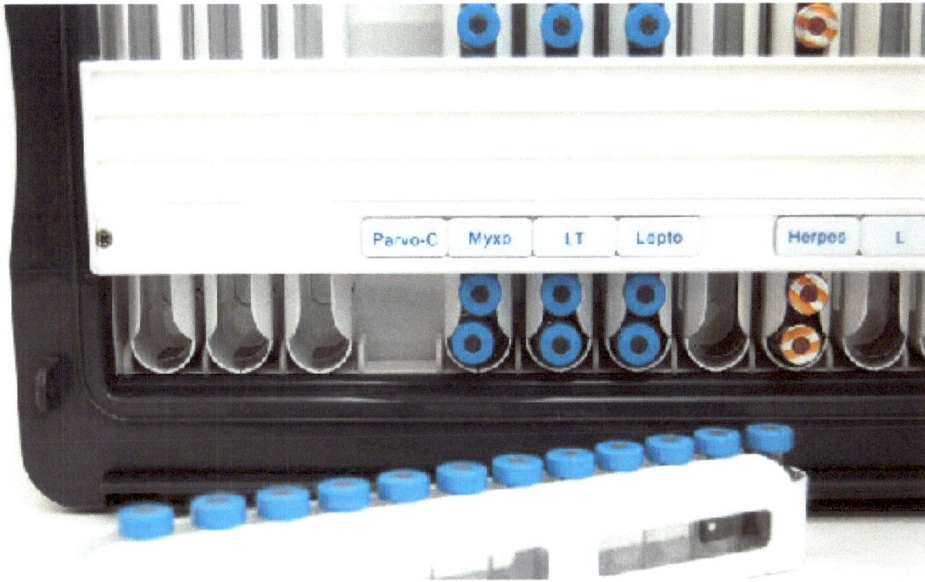

Manufacturer/Designer

Design Bridge London
18 Clerkenwell CloseLondon
EC1R 0QNUnited Kingdom
T: +44 (0)20 7814 9922
F: +44 (0)20 7814 9024
Email: sales_london@designbridge.com

Innovative branded chiller for veterinary vaccines.

To be 100% effective, vaccines must be kept at optimum temperature until the moment they are administered, so this was a prime concern.

It is studied that in most vets' surgeries, time-pressured regimes led to vaccines sitting un-refrigerated for hours before being injected, risking the health of customers' pets.

Using innovative chiller technology, a slim, portable, wall-mounted unit with a simple, bespoke refilling system is designed.

For vets: quick, easy selection and removal, better stock management and a guarantee of optimum temperature.

PHARMA PACKAGING INNOVATIONS

Manufacturer/Designer

Neutroplast, and its subsidiary firm BeyonDevices

To make sure that pharmaceutical packaging is a little bit easier to use for those who most need it, a new "Senior Friendly" jar and closure concept has been developed

The ergonomic shape of the jar and closure is designed to offer a better grip.

The closure remains, however, childresistant. A child's hand, which is smaller, less coordinated, and incapable of effectively gripping the closure, encounters too much resistance to be able to open it.

A hand which is the size of an adult's must be used to open the container, which surprisingly makes all the difference,meaning grandma or grandpa can keep

his or her pills in the medicine cabinet without fear of having young ones getting at them.

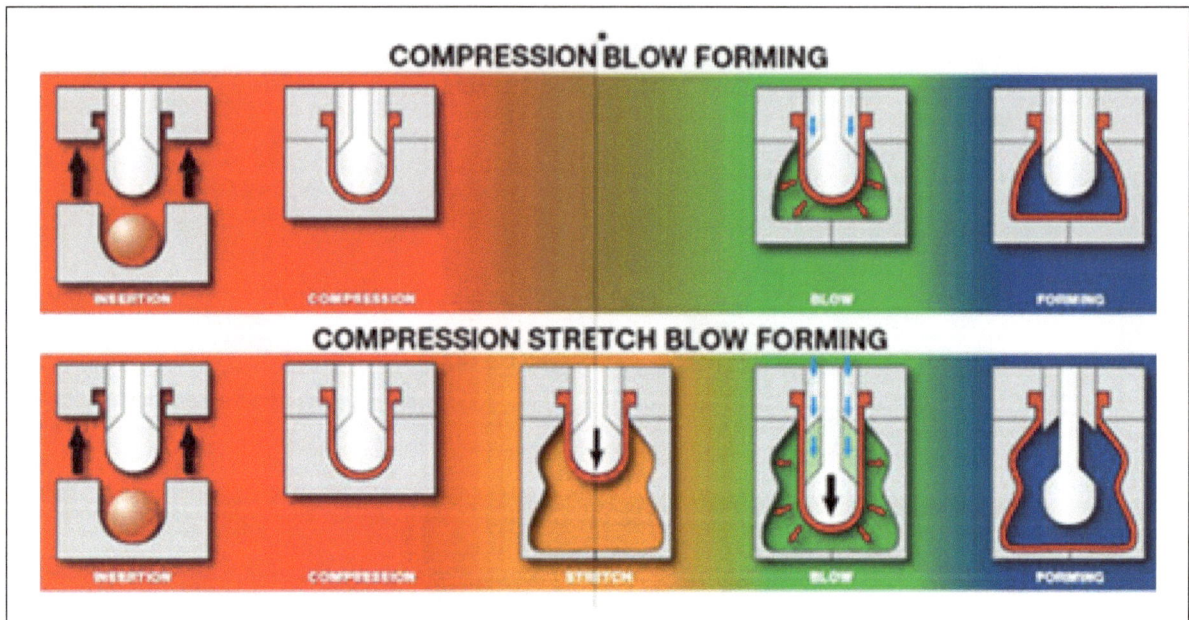

COMPRESSION BLOW FORMING

INSERTION   COMPRESSION   BLOW   FORMING

COMPRESSION STRETCH BLOW FORMING

INSERTION   COMPRESSION   STRETCH   BLOW   FORMING

Manufacturer/Designer

Amcor Rigid Plastics - India Private L
Gat No.119 - 123 , Dhanore
Village, Alandi - Markal Road
Khed Pune 412 105 India
Tel: +91 2135 396000

Single-serve bottles using compression blow forming (CBF) technology, making it the first development to use a CBF machine on a commercial scale. The high density polyethylene bottles are blown on a CBF machine.

Instead of using a manifold for meltdistribution, an extruded shot of resin is transferred directly into the

compression mould, giving producers more control over the quality of the container.

The pre-blow process allows a more consistent and uniform wall thickness by making it easier to separate plastic from the compression core.

The blow process begins immediately after compressing the preform, leaving less chance of material sticking to the metal core rod.

Pharmaceutical

Value Engineering

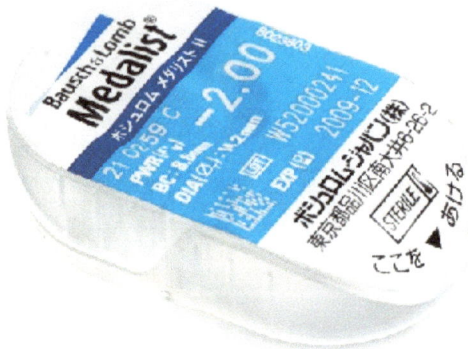

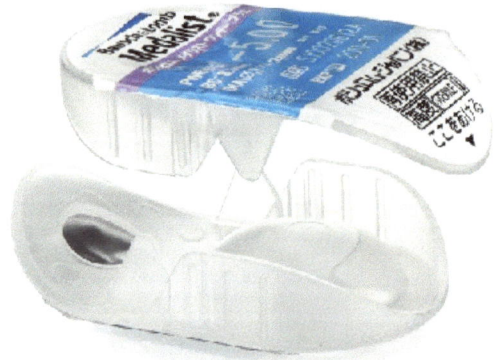

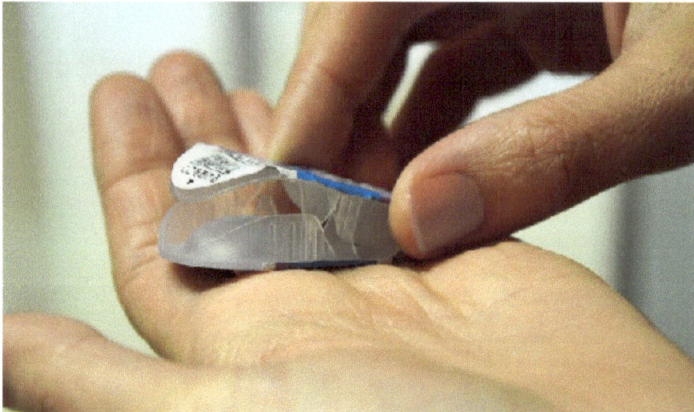

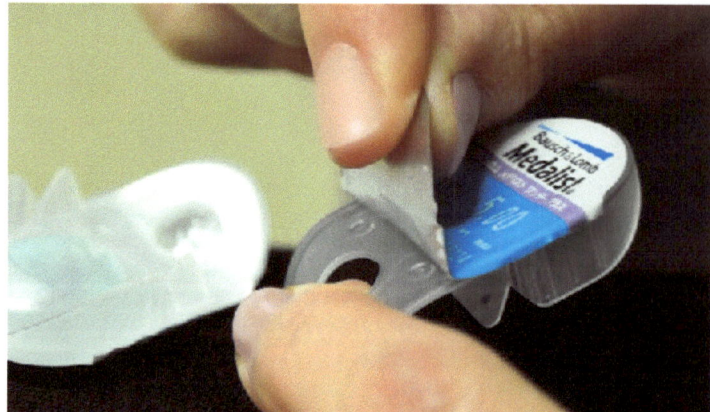

PHARMA PACKAGING INNOVATIONS

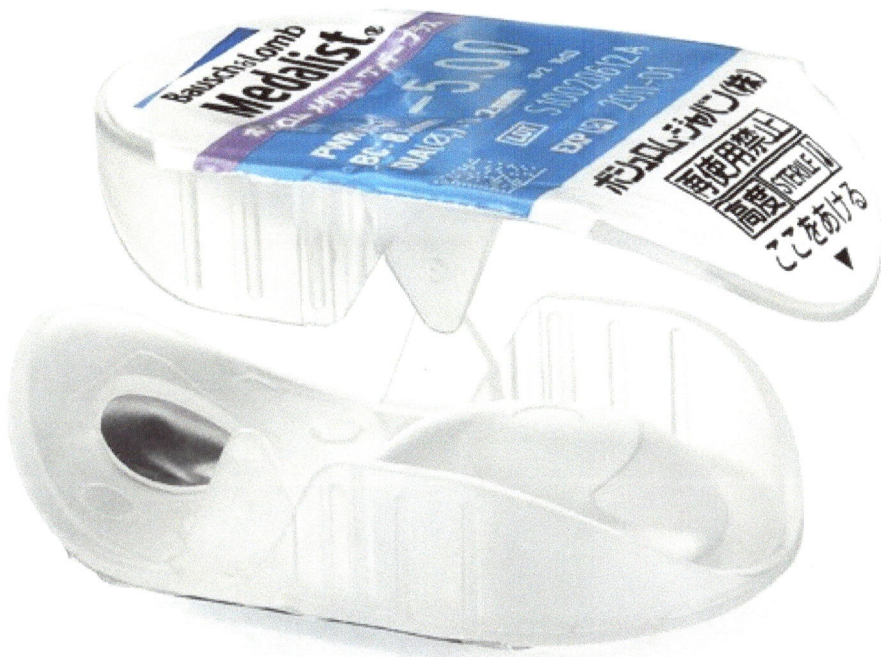

Bausch&Lomb
Medalist
-5.00

Manufacturer/Designer

Design Bridge London
18 Clerkenwell CloseLondon
EC1R 0QNUnited Kingdom
T: +44 (0)20 7814 9922
F: +44 (0)20 7814 9024
Email:sales_london@designbridge.com

Cost-saving product design and harmonisation for international contact lens brand

Production rates increased by 400% and they cut their freight costs by 60%.

This new design also reduced use of materials such as plastic, polyester and aluminium foil - in some cases by 100%.

For consumers, the click-together double pack is intuitive to use and easy to handle, carry and open, inviting brand loyalty.

This handy, cost-effective little pack even takes up half as much space on the shelf and can be recycled.

Material Shift (Glass to Plastic)

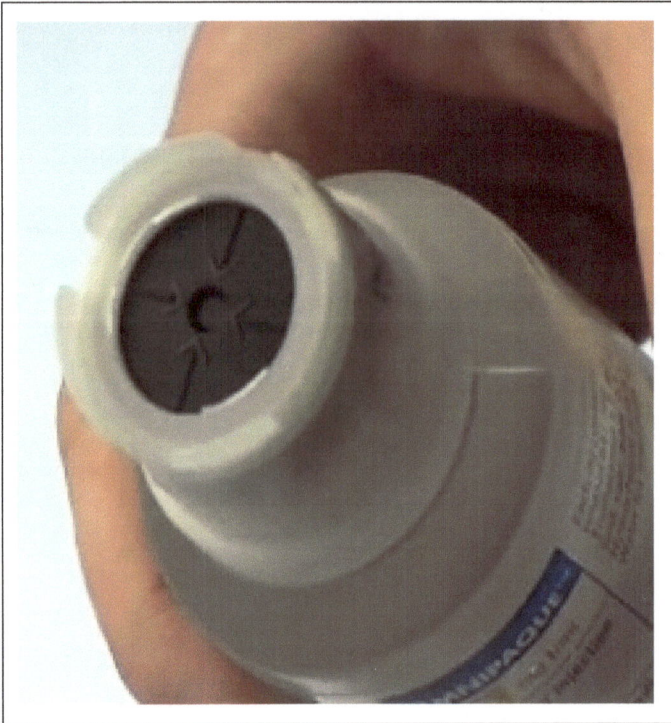

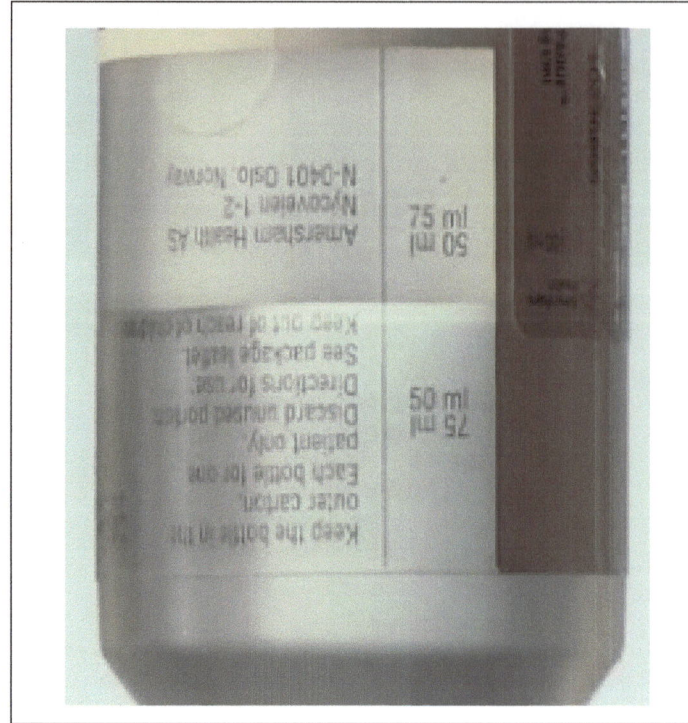

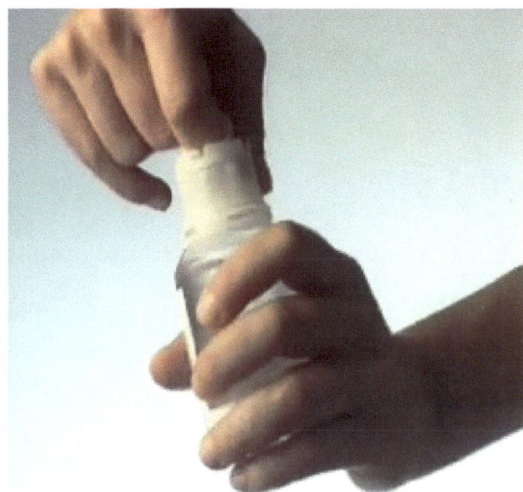

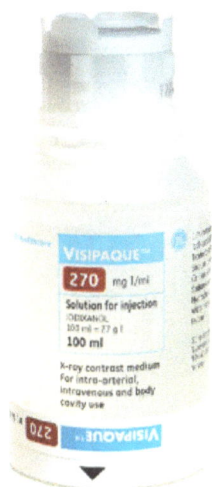

Manufacturer/Designer

GE Plastics BV, Plasticslaan 1,
4612 PX, Bergen op Zoom,
The Netherlands
Tel: +31 (0)164 246457
Fax: +31 (0)164 291652

Designed to minimise the hazards that may occur while opening glass bottles.

The polypropylene bottle removes risk of injuries from glass breakages. While the easy-open polypropylene ring pull avoids cuts from sharp metal edges

Also PP have environment benefits as it uses 16% less energy, releases 60% less SO_2, emits 46% less CO_2 and gives off 75% less ethylene

Unbreakable bottles require less secondary packaging, further reducing your carbon footprint

Simultaneously an interesting label placement is done that allows reading at any angle

Important information is repeated in upside down

PHARMA PACKAGING INNOVATIONS

Pharmaceutical

Compliance Packaging

PHARMA PACKAGING INNOVATIONS

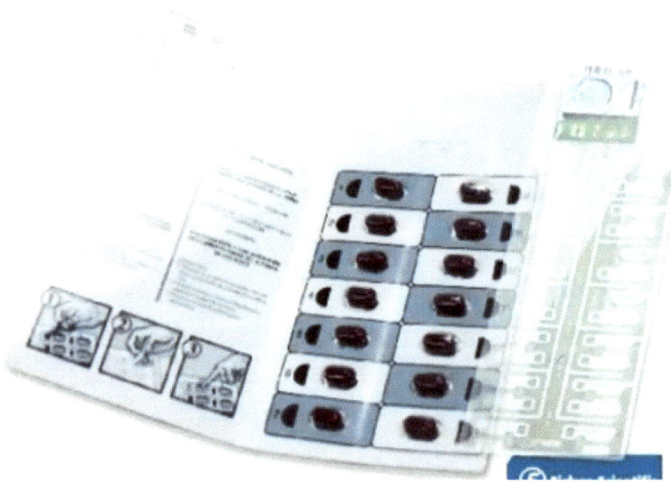

01:00 PM

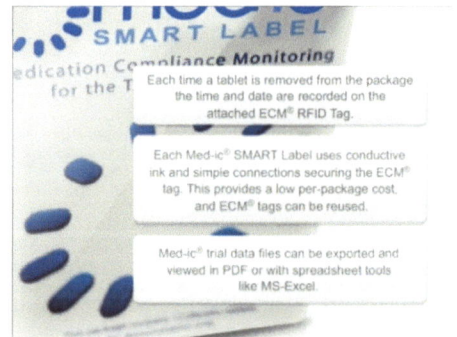

SMART LABEL

edication Compliance Monitoring
for the T

Each time a tablet is removed from the package the time and date are recorded on the attached ECM® RFID Tag.

Each Med-ic® SMART Label uses conductive ink and simple connections securing the ECM® tag. This provides a low per-package cost, and ECM® tags can be reused.

Med-ic® trial data files can be exported and viewed in PDF or with spreadsheet tools like MS-Excel.

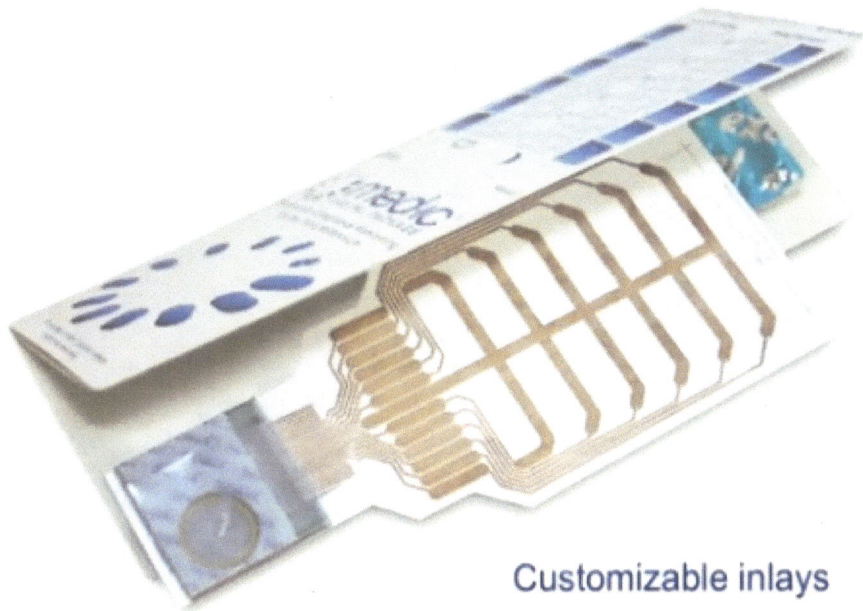

Customizable inlays

Manufacturer/Designer

Information Mediary Corp.
(IMC)2259 Gladwin CrescentOttawa,
Ontario, CanadaK1B 4K9Joanne Watters
jwatters@informationmediary.com
Tel: 613-745-8400 ext 404

The Med-ic® ECM (Electronic ComplianceMonitor) stick-on paper label for medication blisters that provides a disposable packaging.

Med-ic records the time when the patient breaks through the package triggering an event the Med-ic grid traces. The event (time it was broken and pills removed) are stored on the ECM Tag.

The ECM can be read using a smart device, calling into the Med-ic application, a NFC (near field communication), an RFID Reader.

The Med-ic ECM solution uses patented printed sensors of non-toxic, conductive inks printed directly on standard paper label stock.

Med-ic smart labels are completely compatible with standard pharmaceutical heat and cold sealing processes.

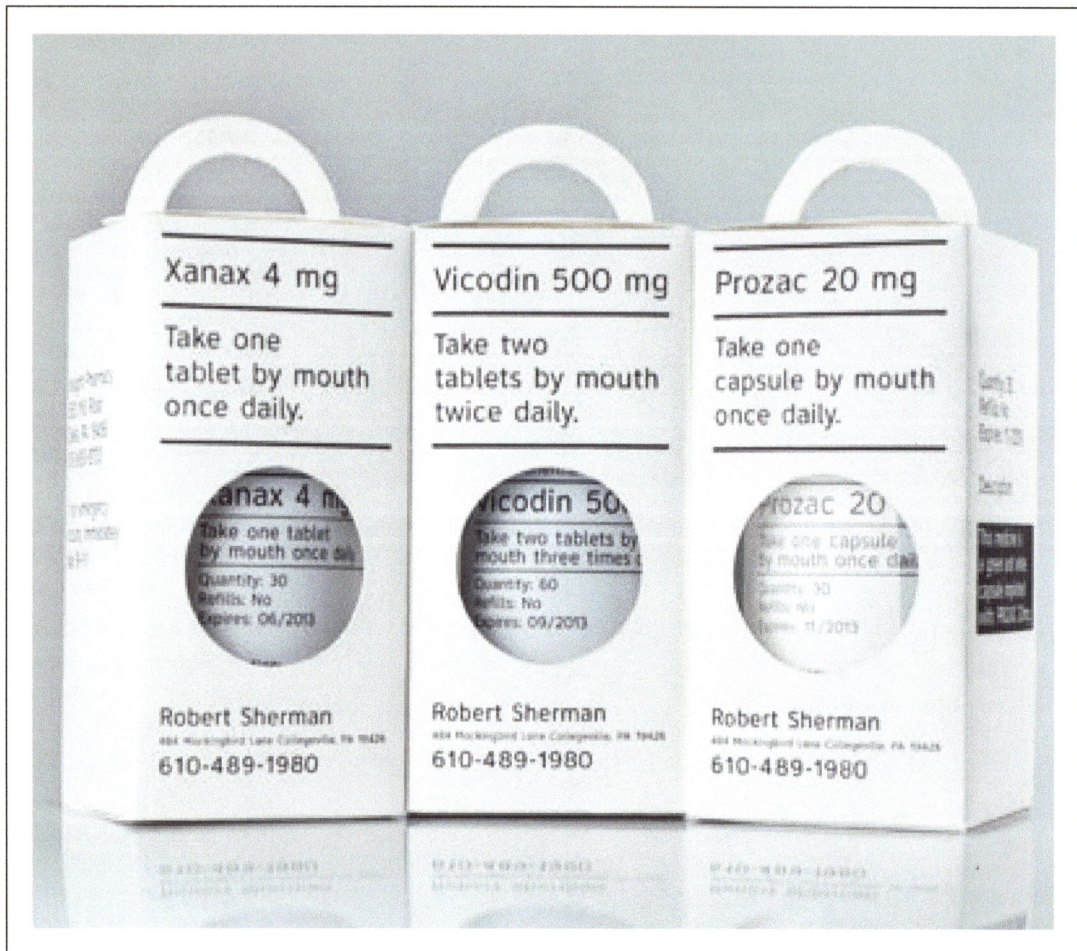

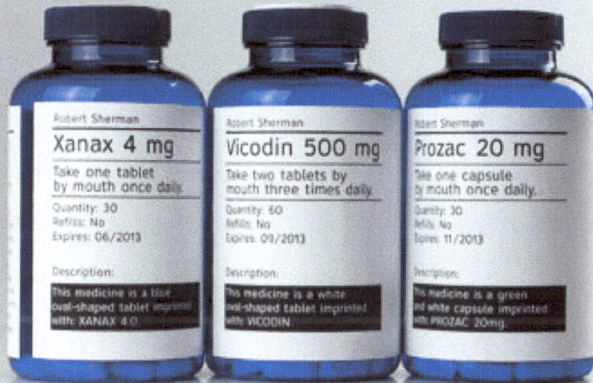

Manufacturer/Designer

Nolato Jaycare (Portsmouth)
Walton Road Farlington Portsmouth.
PO6 1TS United Kingdom
Tel.: +44 (0)2392 370 102
Fax.: +44 (0)2392 380 314
info@nolato.com

The single most important aspect of design is the incorporation of texture into the caps of the prescription bottles.

This aspect is essential to helping "low vision" individuals take their medication

The important part of this idea is that every texture has to be different for every patient, so that they can learn to associate a texture with a certain medication.

This texture aspect of the design allows the user to handle the bottle for a longer period of time, which encourages familiarity.

One of the other important aspects to my design solution was the choice of an appropriate typeface.

This idea was to use repetition in order to clearly get information across to the viewer as often as possible. The color scheme of this prescription identity was chosen to most enhance the readability and ledgeability for "low vision" individuals.

PHARMA PACKAGING INNOVATIONS

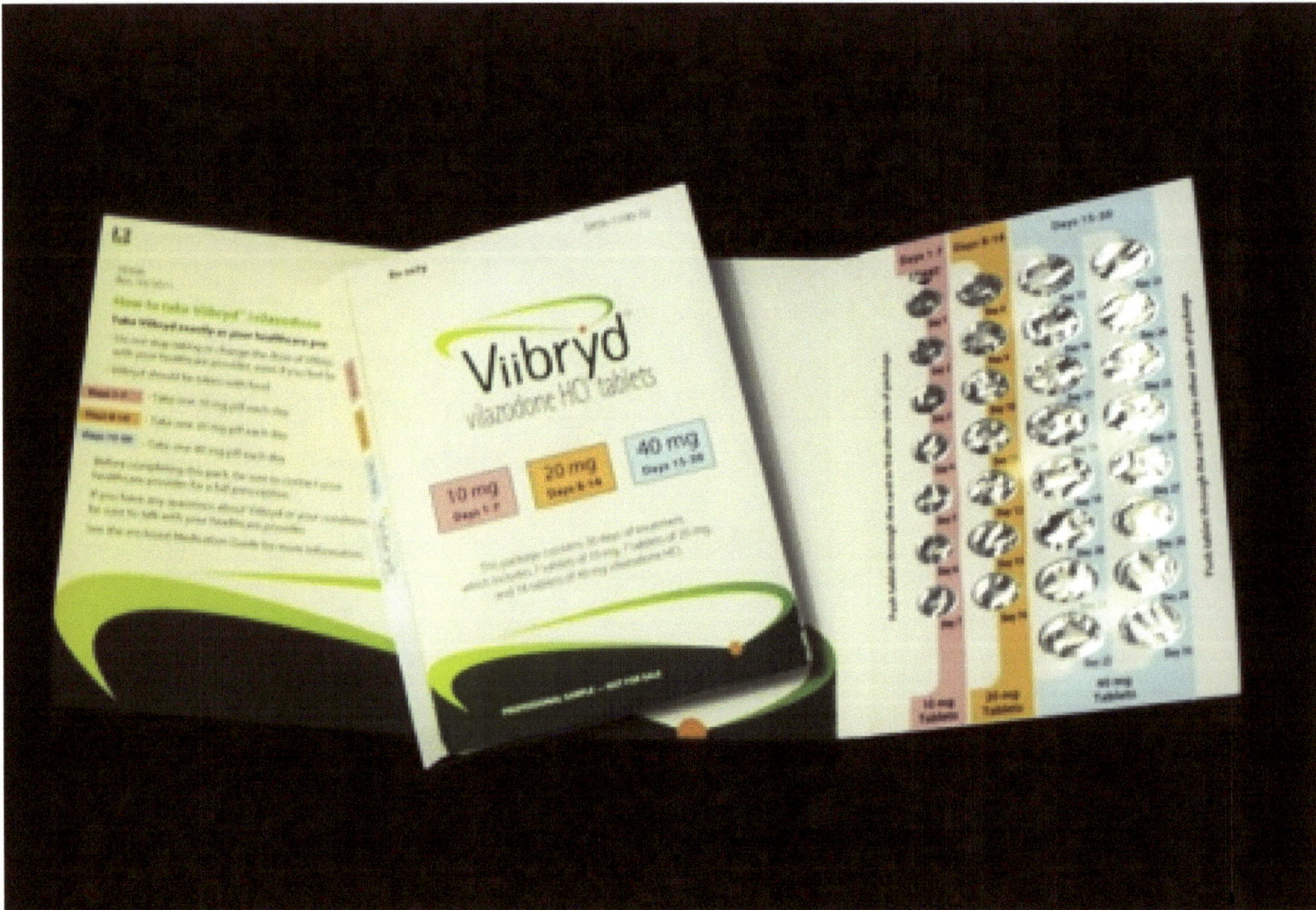

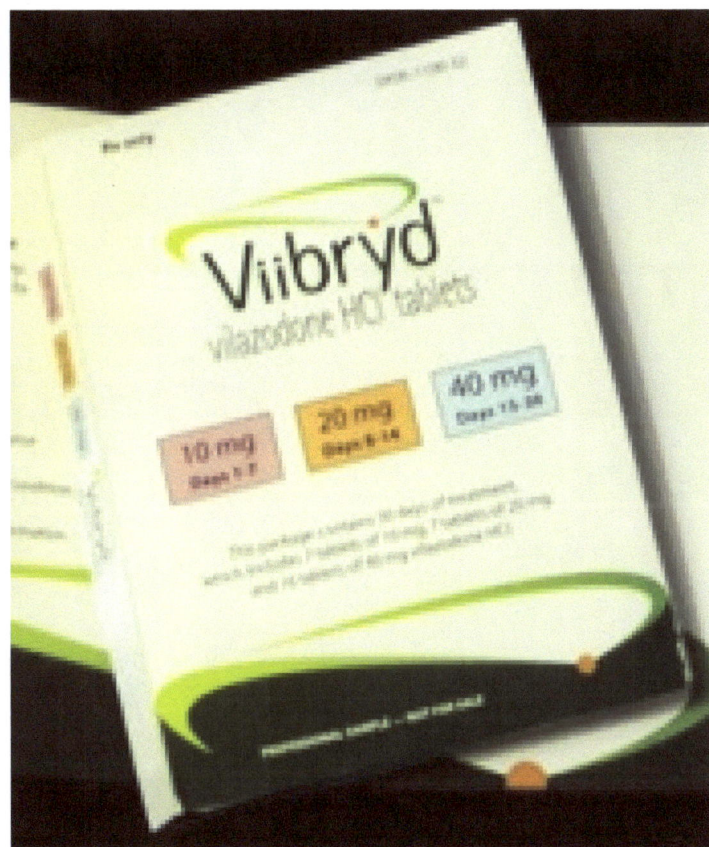

Manufacturer/Designer

AndersonBrecon
4545 ASSEMBLY DRIVE
ROCKFORD, IL 61109 USA
+1 815 484 8900

This package's graphics use color to help patients follow complicated instructions for doses that vary for three different time periods during the month.

Compared to the other packs, has to deliver more complicated instructions because the doseor med varies for three different time periods during the month.

That presents the only real challenge to the patient.

This patient compliance/adherence pack is enjoyable to unfold, and the graphics do a terrific job in their use of colour to help the patient follow his or her drug regimen.

Instructions are easy to access, pills look easy to use,

PHARMA PACKAGING INNOVATIONS

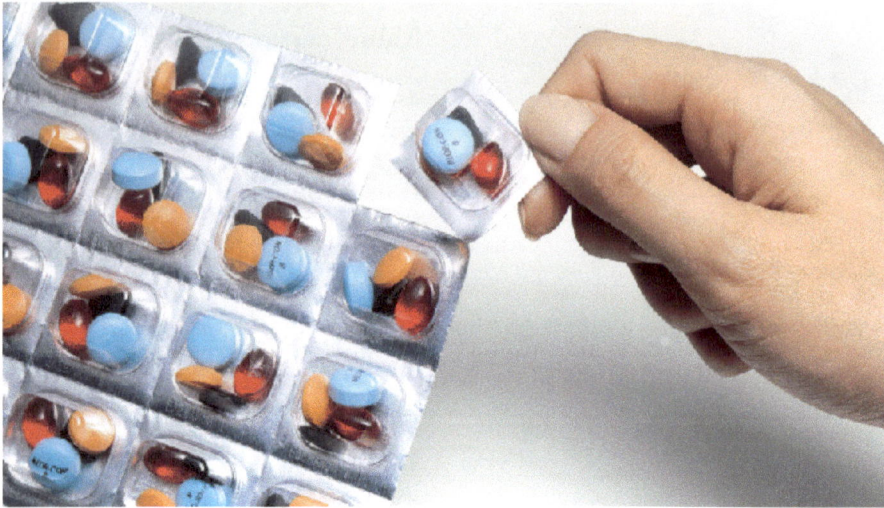

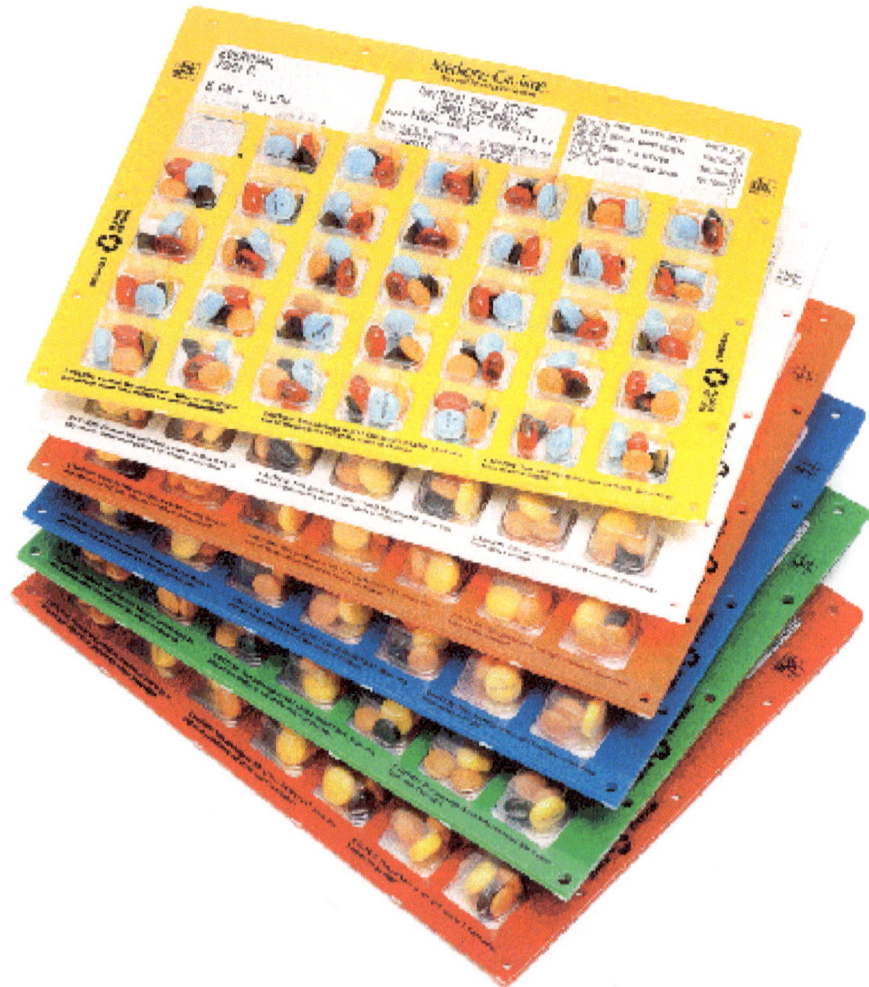

PHARMA PACKAGING INNOVATIONS

Manufacturer/Designer

Nolato Jaycare (Portsmouth)
Walton Road Farlington Portsmouth.
PO6 1TS United Kingdom
Tel.: +44 (0)2392 370 102
Fax.: +44 (0)2392 380 314
info@nolato.com

Compliance pack at hospital/doctor's level

While prescribing a combination of dosage the doctor can pack multi pills in a single blister

Readymade cardboard and blister pockets are available

Option to mention day, time or even dosage duration

This can solve issues that arises due to medical error

Quick-release package" is a single-sidedsystem that permits quick removal of the pill where punch-through opening is not an option. Again, each blister cavity can hold up to six pills.

This is not at customer's end but at prescriber's end

Pharmaceutical

Technology

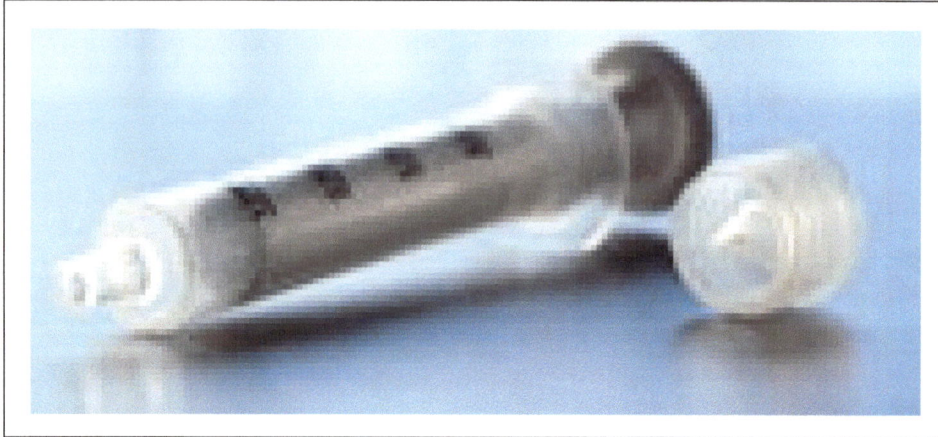

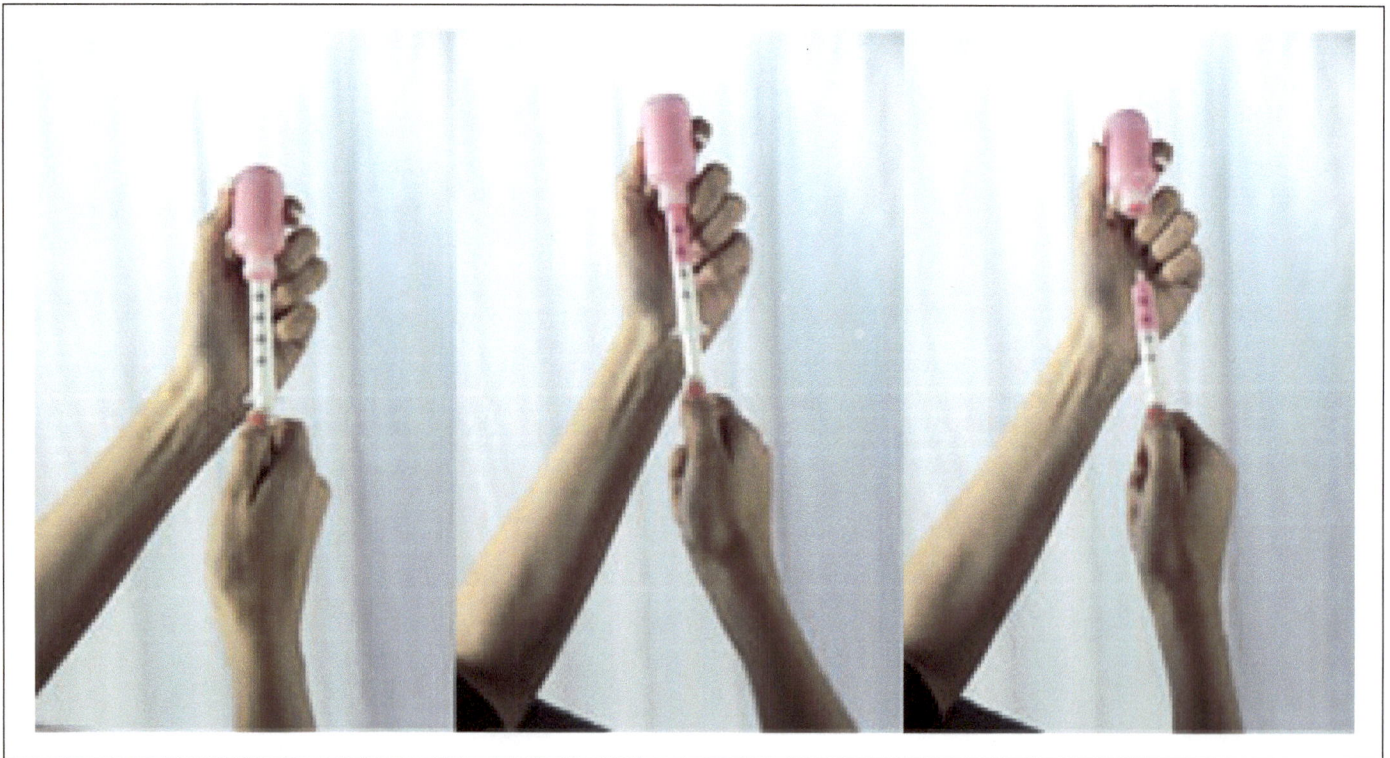

Manufacturer/Designer

One Comar Place.
Buena, NJ 08310-9901
Tel: (800) 962-6627
information@comar.com

Prevents accidental ingestion, by safely securing liquid medications

Superior valved design tightly seals after repeated use

Tight seal prevents evaporation, spillage and ontamination

Single molded valve component, prevents contamination associated with multiple processes.

No septum or liner needed, reducing parts and eliminating potential choking hazard

Vented valve relieves pressure and eases ability to withdraw product

Adapter securely connected to custom container finish with interlocking ribs

Child Resistant feature. Syringe has a one-piece plunger and patented wiper design

Syringe delivers accurate and precisedosage

PHARMA PACKAGING INNOVATIONS

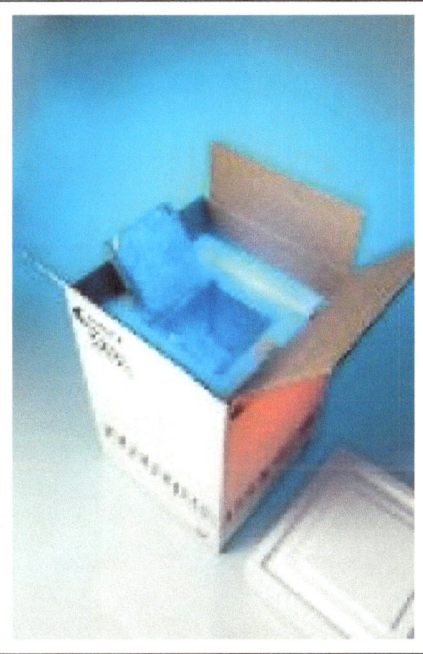

Manufacturer/Designer

Stanbridge Road Leighton Buzzard
Bedfordshire LU7 4QQ United Kingdom
Tel: +44 1525 243770
Fax: +44 1525 243779
cool.info@sca.com
www.cool-logistics.com

Innovative use of alufoil to help create a packaging solution for sensitive drugs which are reliant on correct temperatures being maintained during transit.

ZeoCool does not use cool packs to freeze or cool the contents.

It is a self-contained unit which uses a technology held within an aluminium casing to enable the six side interior payload area to produce evaporative cooling or heating.

No external energy sources are needed and it is the only system to utilise a phase change of liquid to gas

Manufacturer/Designer

Entropy Solutions, Inc.
USA 151 Cheshire Lane, Suite 400,
Plymouth MN 55441
Phone: 952-941-0306
Fax: 952-944-6893
http://www.puretemp.com

GREENBOX™ reusable thermal management system employs a total system approach to assuring that products will arrive at their destination uncompromised.

It is powered by PureTemp™, Entropy's renewable based, non-toxic phase change technology, which keep contents at the right temperature for more than 120 hours.

The Thermal-Lok™ panels have insulating values ten times that of expanded polystryrene (EPS).

The system components are reusable, and the end of life, the outer shell and Thermal-Lok™ panels are ground for reuse in new systems.

Manufacturer/Designer

NEOPAC THE TUBE
Switzerland
+41 317701111
info@neopac.com
www.neopac.com

Trials were carried out on two different groups to test on the one hand child safety and on the other hand accessibility for the elderly by asking to open the tube in 5minutes

Elderly accessibility test was considered passed when at least 90% of the test group had successfully opened and closed the packaging within one minute.

The child-resistant design of the unit dose Twist'n'Use system, allows the closure to be squeezed and turned while the internal pin is released and the liquid or cream can be applied selectively

PHARMA PACKAGING INNOVATIONS

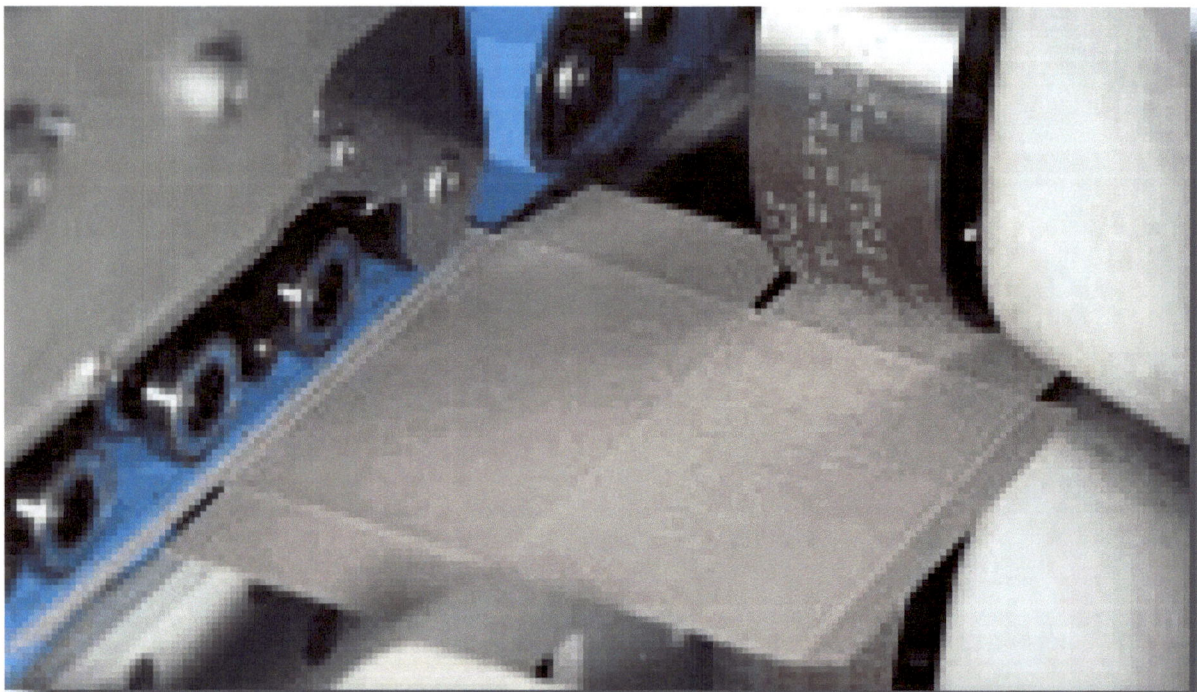

Manufacturer/Designer

RLC | packaging group Germany
Phone: +49 511/16499-49
www.rlc-packaging.com

Smart Braille Solution. where embossing is no longer needs to be done in the die cutting stage

If expedient, it can now also be moved down the production line to the folder-gluer.

The advantage being cartons are individually processed, in contrast to automated die cutters.

Consequently, only one tool is needed instead of one for every "up".

The new rotary process speeds make ready and delivers high-quality, robust Braille dots.

Die cutting capacity, flexibility and productivity are also increased.

PHARMA PACKAGING INNOVATIONS

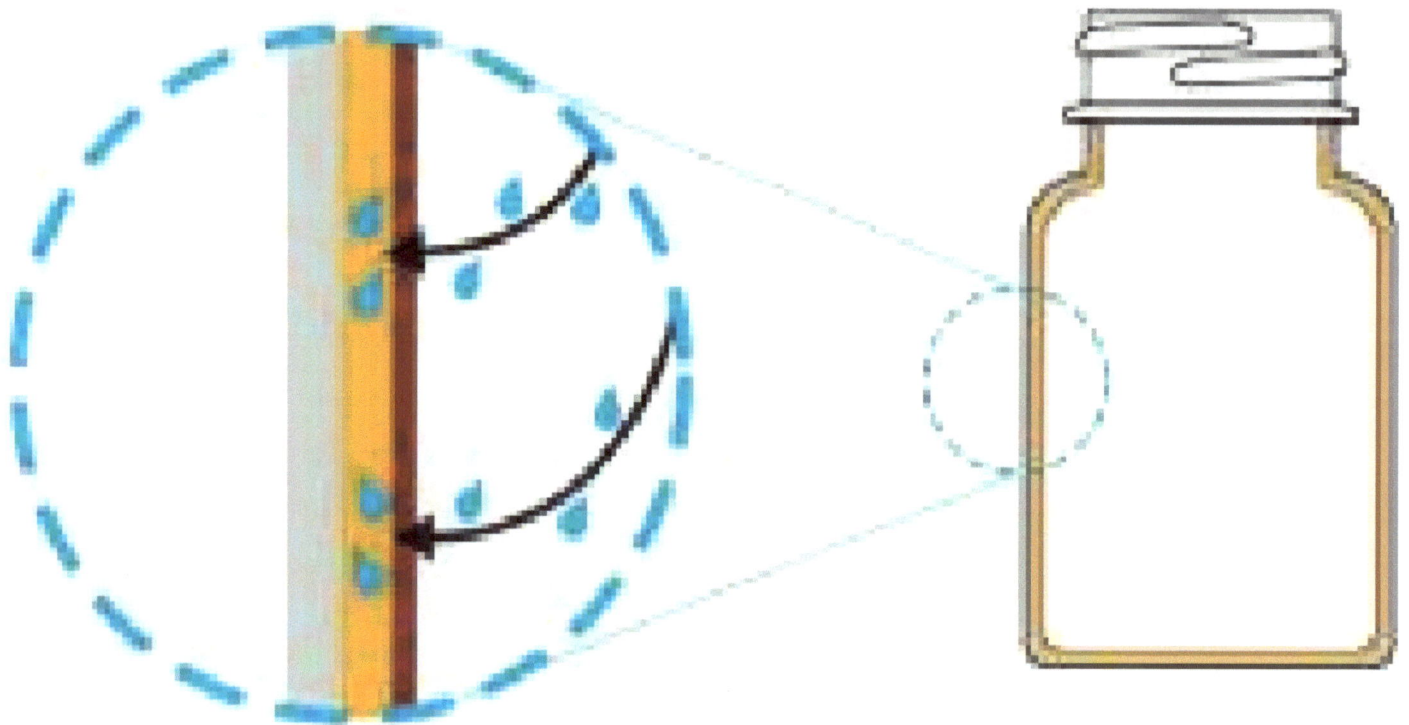

- Outer Layer (HDPE)
- Middle Layer (DryKeep™ Layer)
- Inner Layer (HDPE or LDPE)

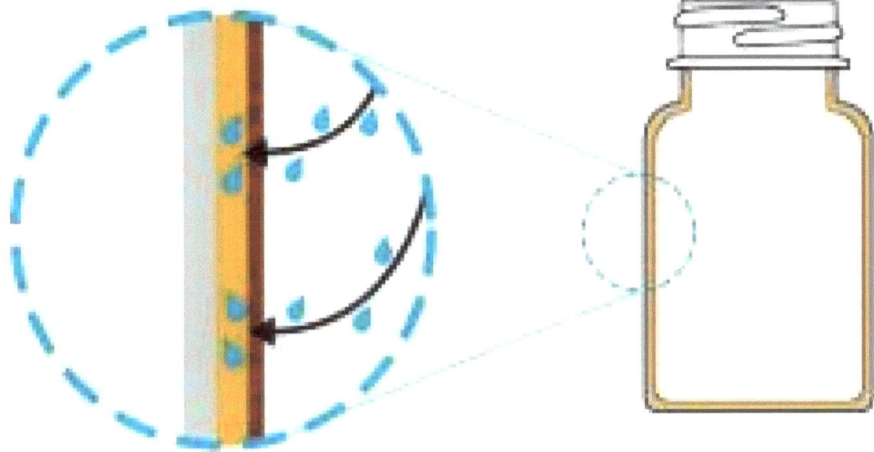

Manufacturer/Designer

TricorBraun
8212 Lackland Rd,
St Louis, MO 63114,
United States
Phone:+1 314-569-3633
http://www.tricorbraun.com

It is a desiccant entrained polymer that can be molded into bottle to maintain the moisture in the shelf life of the product.

Eliminate issues such as dusting, leaking of loose canister or sachetm

Advantage being higher shelf-life of solid Orals in Bottle

Gives value in terms of safety by improving product stability.

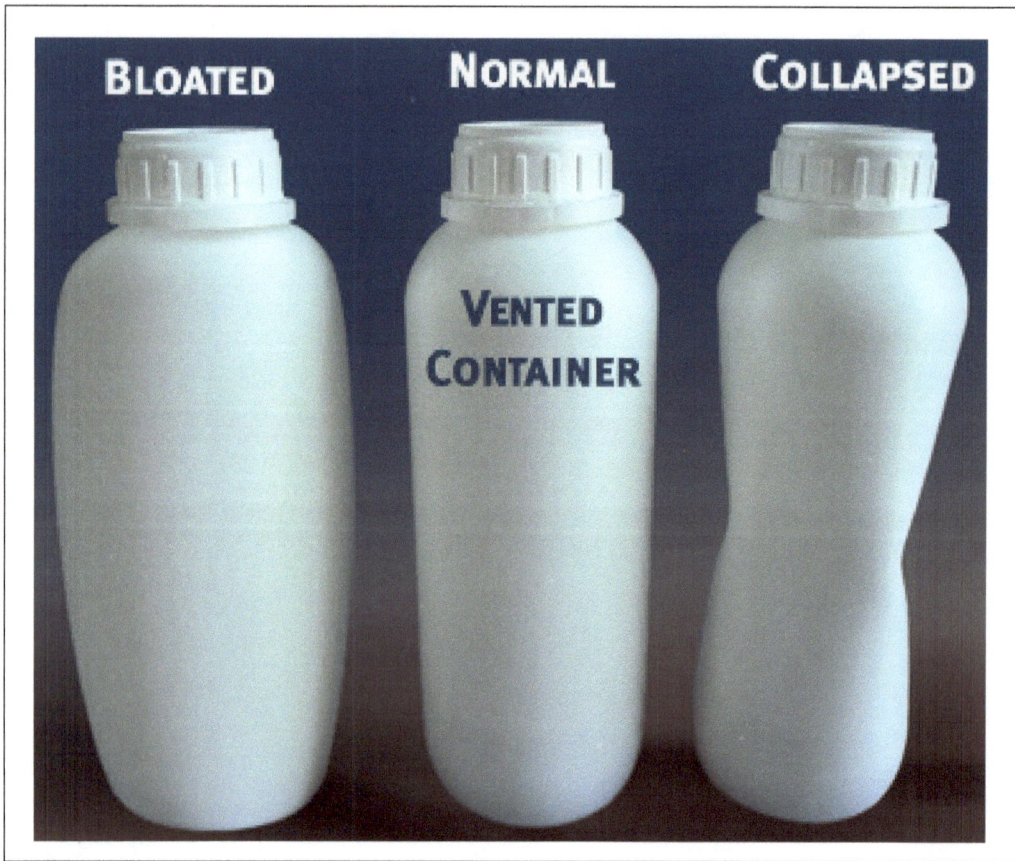

BLOATED   NORMAL   COLLAPSED

VENTED CONTAINER

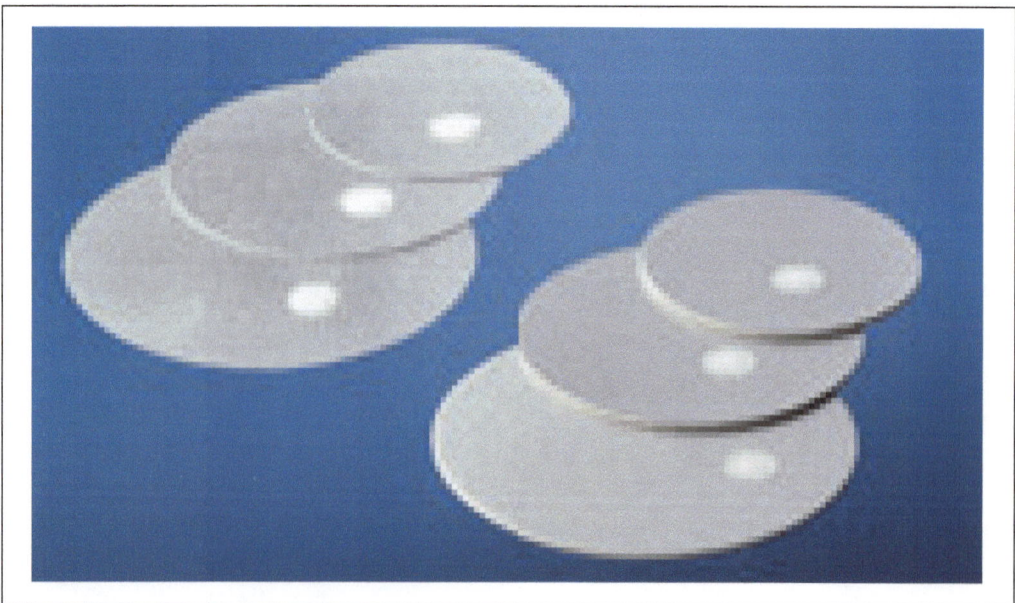

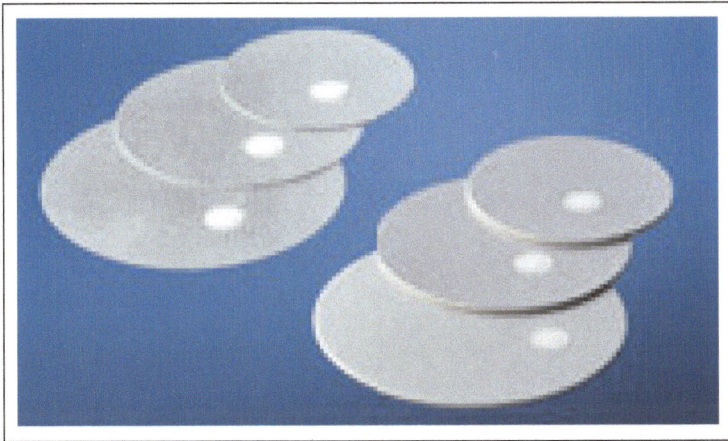

Manufacturer/Designer

GORE Packaging Vents
Phone: 410-506-7787
http://www.gore.com

Vents provided in the induction linerscan be used for the products that generates gases, eg — Amoxycillin

This provides safety by improving stability

The principle is that the through vent,pressure is equalized that prevents containers from bloating or collapsing or leaking

In turn maintains container's integrity

PHARMA PACKAGING INNOVATIONS

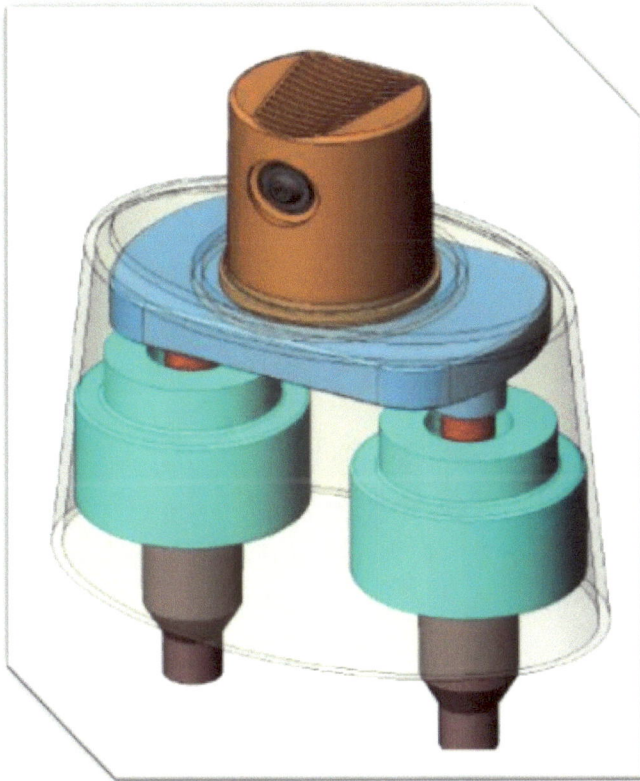

Manufacturer/Designer

Micromixer from HPT
Mr Michael Löffler
Sales Director / Vice President
sales@hpt.info
Tel: +49 (0) 3679/72 606 0
Fax: +49 (0) 3679/72 606 79

For two different semisolid products (e.g. gels)

The products can be mixed to homogeneous system before dispensing.

Provides simplification of dispensing for easy usage

Can be extended to two immiscible products

which needs to be administered together probably with two heads e.g. drug like Benzoyl Peroxide and Clindawvcin

PHARMA PACKAGING INNOVATIONS

100 % germfree
5-fold mechanical protection,
with or without filter system

1 First non-return valve
directly below the orifice
bore

2 Second non-return valve
in the metering chamber

3 Filter element for
contamination-free
ventilation of the container

4 Locked nasal adapter

5 Sealed air path during
storage

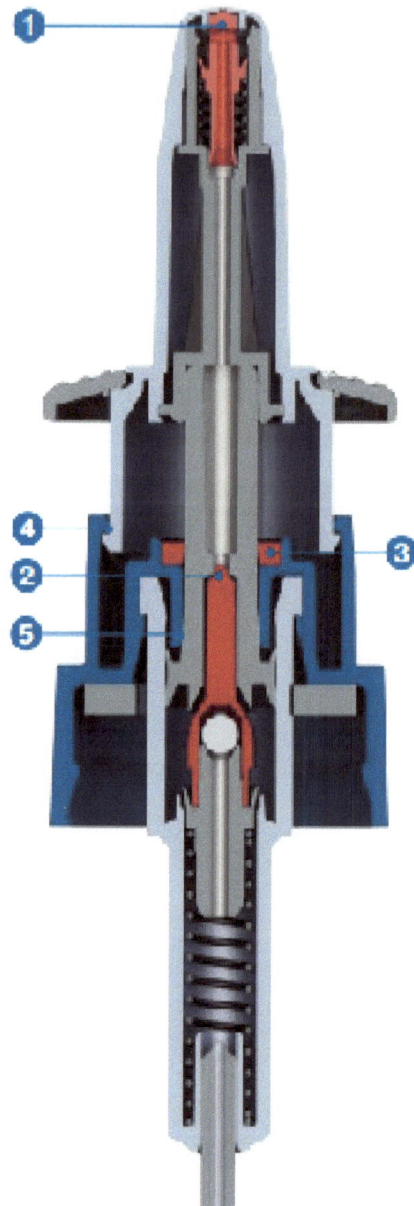

Pump
performance

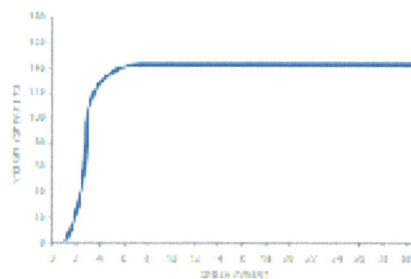

Plume
Geometry

Spray
Pattern

Completely flexible
Can be easily modified for
individual configurations and
delivery amounts

CAP 01   CAP 02

Manufacturer/Designer

MeadWestvaco Calmar Gmbh
Tel. + 49 23 72 5040
E: mwv@mwvhealthcare.com
W: www.mwvhealthcare.com

PFP N (Preservative Free Pump Nasal), is a state-of-the-art preservative-free metered nasal spray pump device

The device can allow you to extend andenhance your brand identity through a product life cycle management strategy

By reformulating to remove a preservative and using a novel delivery method, it may be possible to extend commercial exclusivity.

Germ free, uses non-silver spring with no oligodynamic components.

Shut-off valve to avoid contamination, filter system for venting air (non-venting version without filter system available)

PHARMA PACKAGING INNOVATIONS

Manufacturer/Designer

Aisapack SA
Switzerland
+ 41 24 4820 600
bacomex@aisapack.com
www.aisapack.com

The SAESA® laminate tube consists of several components assembled into a high barrier tube.

The tube sleeve comprised of aluminium orplastic barrier laminate is an effective barrier protection.

Using compression moulding, a SAESA® shoulder can be made using Bacomex™ multilayer technology that stops the escape of the aroma and the ingress of the oxygen

By same technology, high barrier PET bottles can also be produced with multilayer preforms.

Pharmaceutical

Concepts

PHARMA PACKAGING INNOVATIONS

Independent Remedies

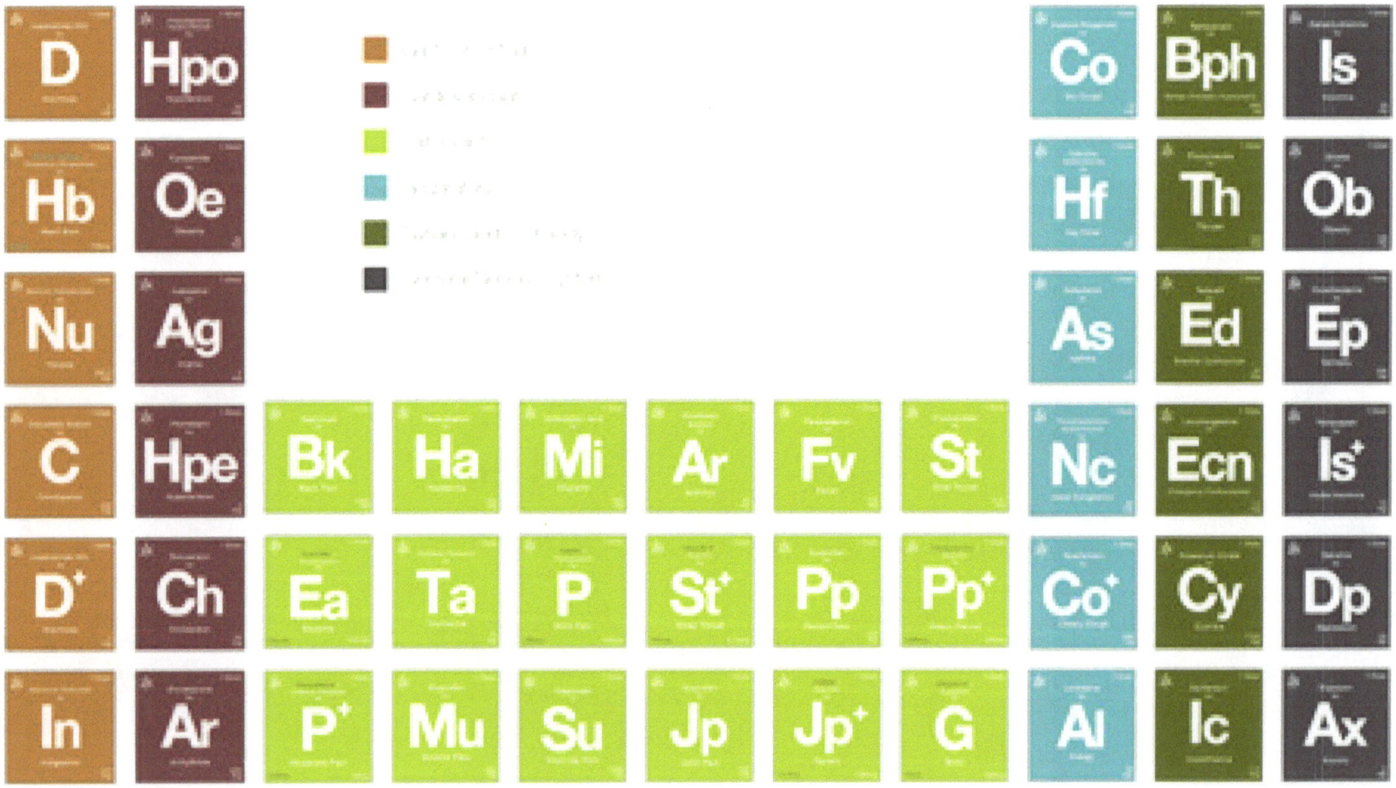

Manufacturer/Designer

**Designed by Alex Lee,
University of Leeds, UK**

A simple, streamlined and instructional packaging typology lets doctors easily inform the ill about their prescriptions for OTC drugs.

A structured user experience, communicated in a clear, concise, and understandable manor, accessible to all.

Individual medications can be found on a chart that looks like the periodic table, and each separate icon corresponds to the exact appearance of the medicines' labels.

With a goal for encouraging the responsible administration and consumption of pills and elixirs,

Independent Remedies incorporates child resistant wrapping and a system of QR code scanning for accurate records and additional information.

Tetrahedron Tablet Packaging

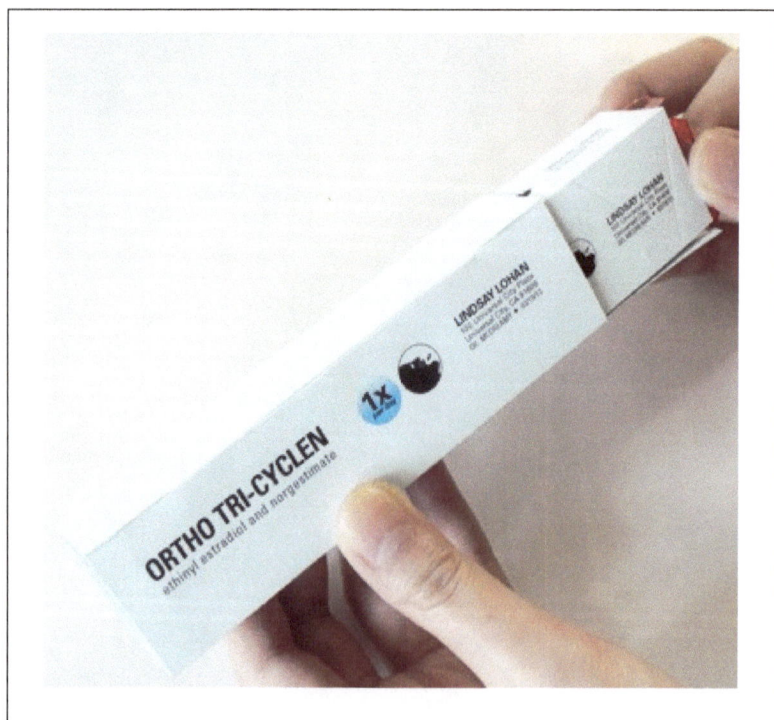

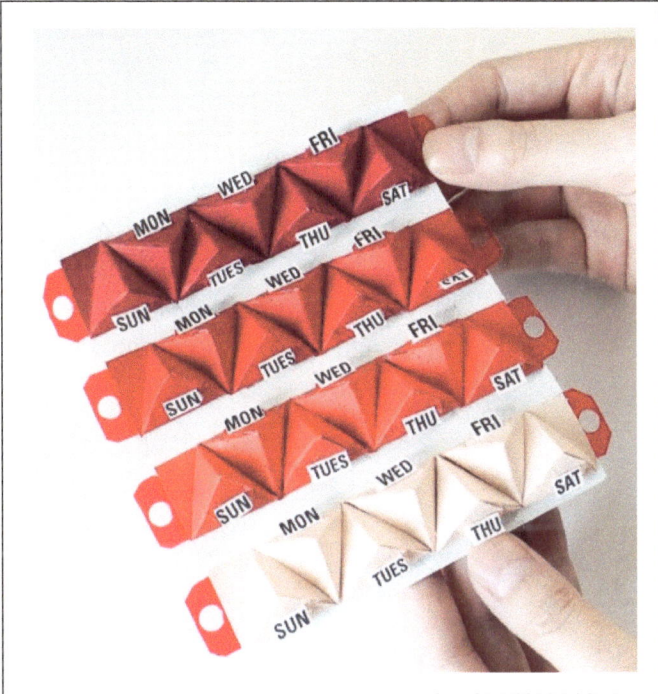

Manufacturer/Designer

University of Washington Seattle
J Seattle, WA, USA

Calendar Packaging for Pharmaceutical

Ease of compliance and error free

Each row is perforated to take on the go

Take out pills from outer layer

Additional information within the packaging

Each tetrahedron is perforated at the tip.

The days of the weeks are tabs to tear the tip off and grab the pill held within the package.

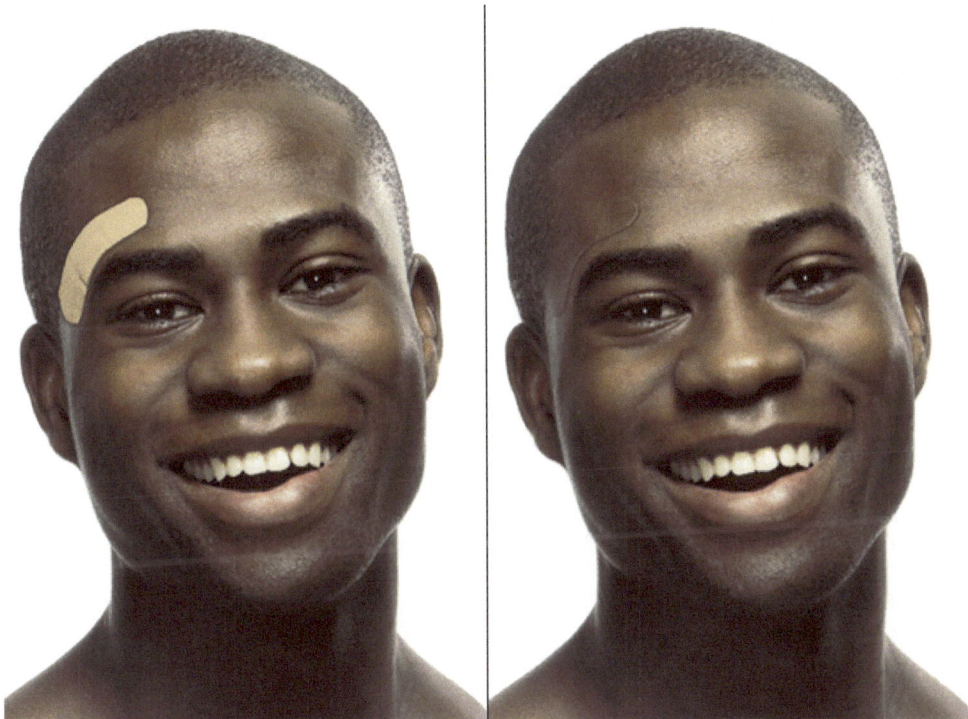

Manufacturer/Designer

Designers Xue Xing Wu, Zi Yu Li, Yue Hua Zhu and Zhi Qiang Wang

The bandage is designed to blend into the wearer's skin, providing a seamless concealed covering.

The 'Chameleon Bandageis' keeps your wounds protected while staying undercover

The invisible band-aid could revolutionizemedical practices and make healing a less embarrassing process.

Reconstructive surgery often requires awkwardly placed dressings and the same science could potentially be used for these larger gauzes.

While the exact science of this miracle band-aid has yet to be revealed, it is likely to be the result of a

PHARMA PACKAGING INNOVATIONS

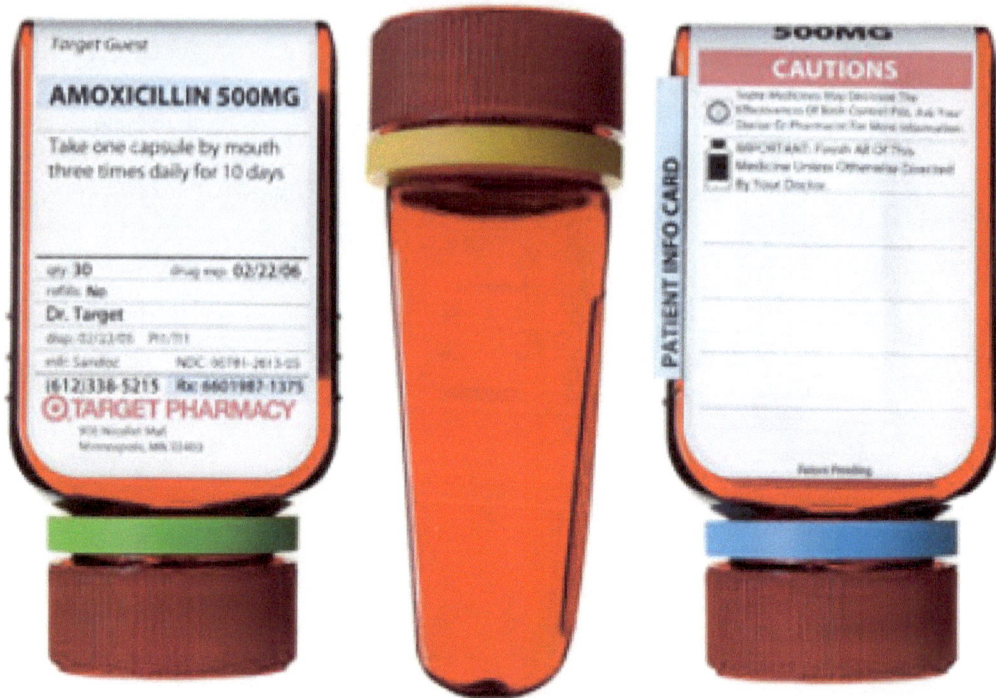

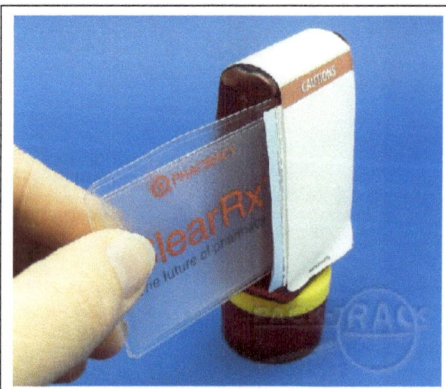

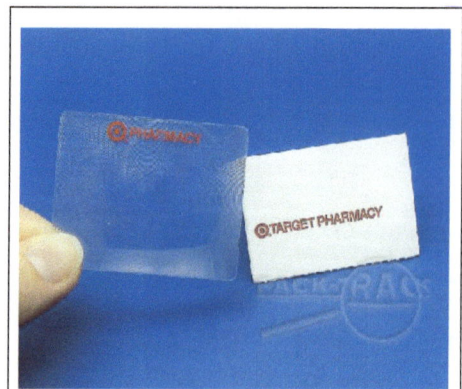

PHARMA PACKAGING INNOVATIONS

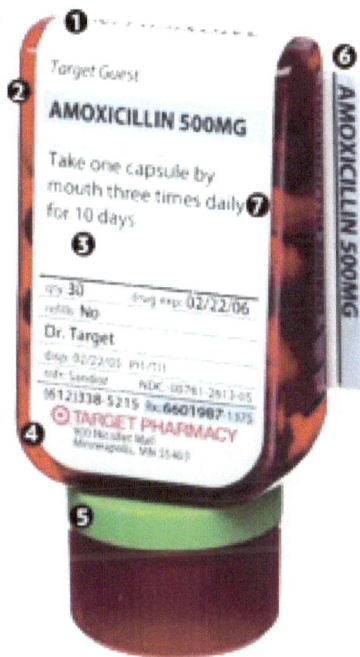

AMOXICILLIN 500MG

Target Guest

Take one capsule by mouth three times daily for 10 days

qty 30   drug exp: 02/22/06
refills: No
Dr. Target

TARGET PHARMACY

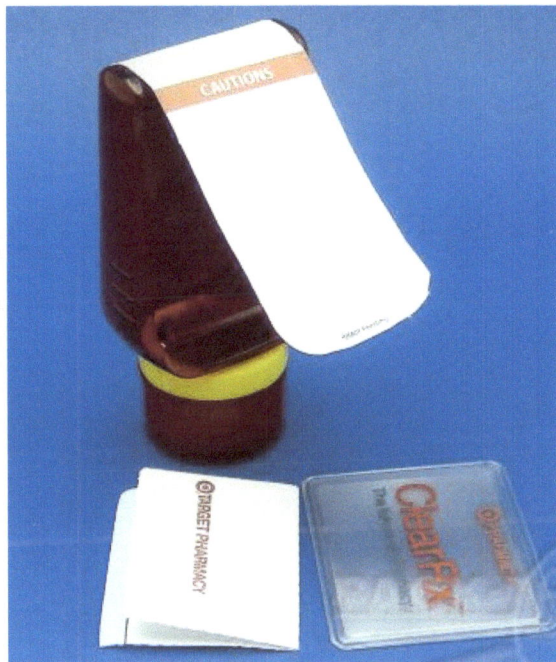

Manufacturer/Designer

School of Visual Arts in New York City student Deborah Adler Adopted by Target Corporation (with refinements by industrial designer Klaus Rosburg)

Round amber coloured bottles have been given an inverted shape

For distinguishing, different colored neck rings are provided.

Also the bottles are flattened out so patients can read labels without rotating the package.

On the back panel, crucial information can be printed

An additional fflexible plastics magnifying device has been provided that magnifies the small text to improve readability

Magnifier fits behind pack label & patient care card. It improve patient compliance for those with poor sight to read labels

Prescription Product targeted to visually poor patient e.g. elderly patient

PHARMA PACKAGING INNOVATIONS

Pharmaceutical

Anti - Counterfeiting

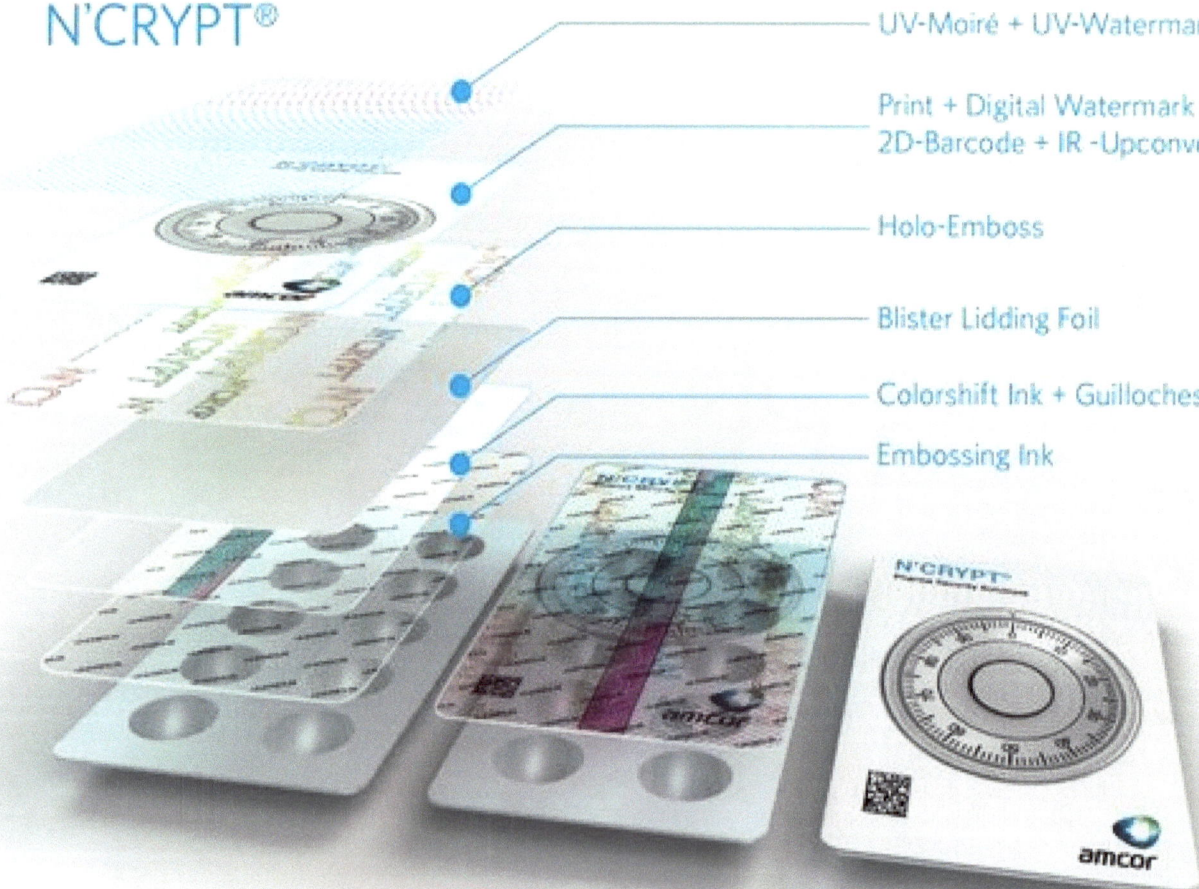

N'CRYPT®

- UV-Moiré + UV-Watermark
- Print + Digital Watermark
- 2D-Barcode + IR -Upconverter
- Holo-Emboss
- Blister Lidding Foil
- Colorshift Ink + Guilloches + Microtext
- Embossing Ink

Ncrypt web

Manufacturer/Designer

Amcor
Medical Packaging Sales
"C-519, Sector-19 " Noida
Uttar Pradesh 201301 "India"
Tel: 91 120 2524781
Fax: +91 120 2524067
http://www.amcor.com

An Innovative and Proven Approach in Delivering Patient Safety for Supply Chain Integrity and Pharmaceutical Brand Protection

Layers of Overt, Covert and combination counterfeit.

N'CRYPT® Security Solutions represents an Innovative and Proven Approach in Delivering Patient Safety, Supply Chain Integrity and Pharmaceutical Brand Protection

Product ApplicationInhalants

Tablets and capsules

Transdermal patches

Available in Global

PHARMA PACKAGING INNOVATIONS

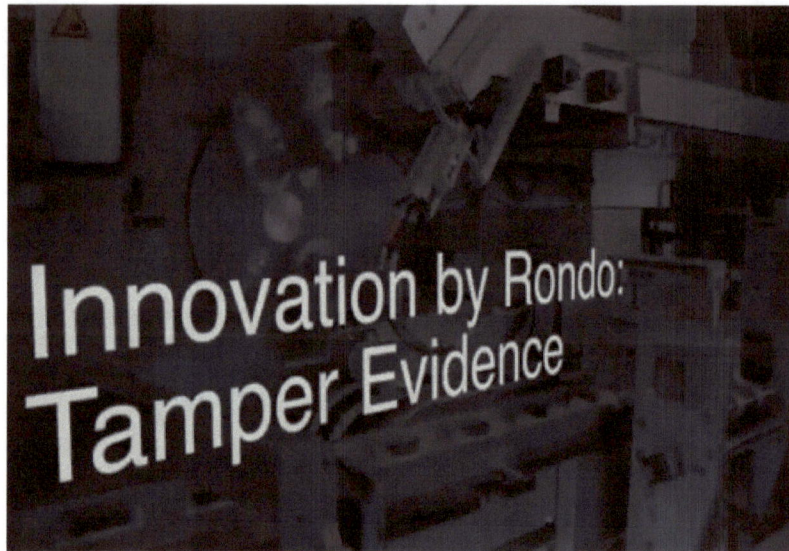

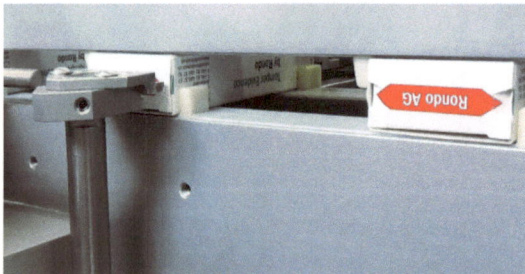
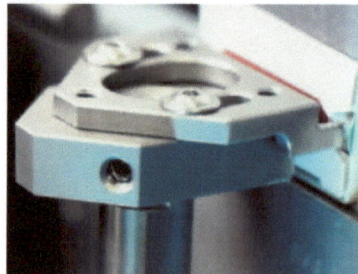
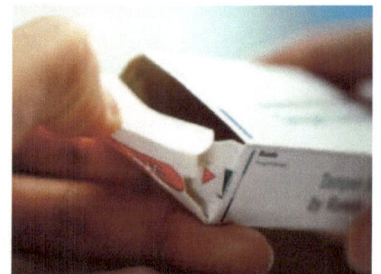

Manufacturer/Designer

Rondo AG Switzerland
T +41 61 486 87 87
sales@rondodruck.ch

Folding box with tamper evidence features first pening verification through perforations in the closing lid and the dust flaps that rip off when the folding box is opened the first time

This solution has the great advantage of being realized solely by converting the carton which makes it completely independent from the use of additional materials such as glue or labels

In addition the folding box remains reclose able at any time

This solution has the great advantage of being realized solely by converting the carton which makes it completely independent from the use of additional materials such as glue or labels.

PHARMA PACKAGING INNOVATIONS

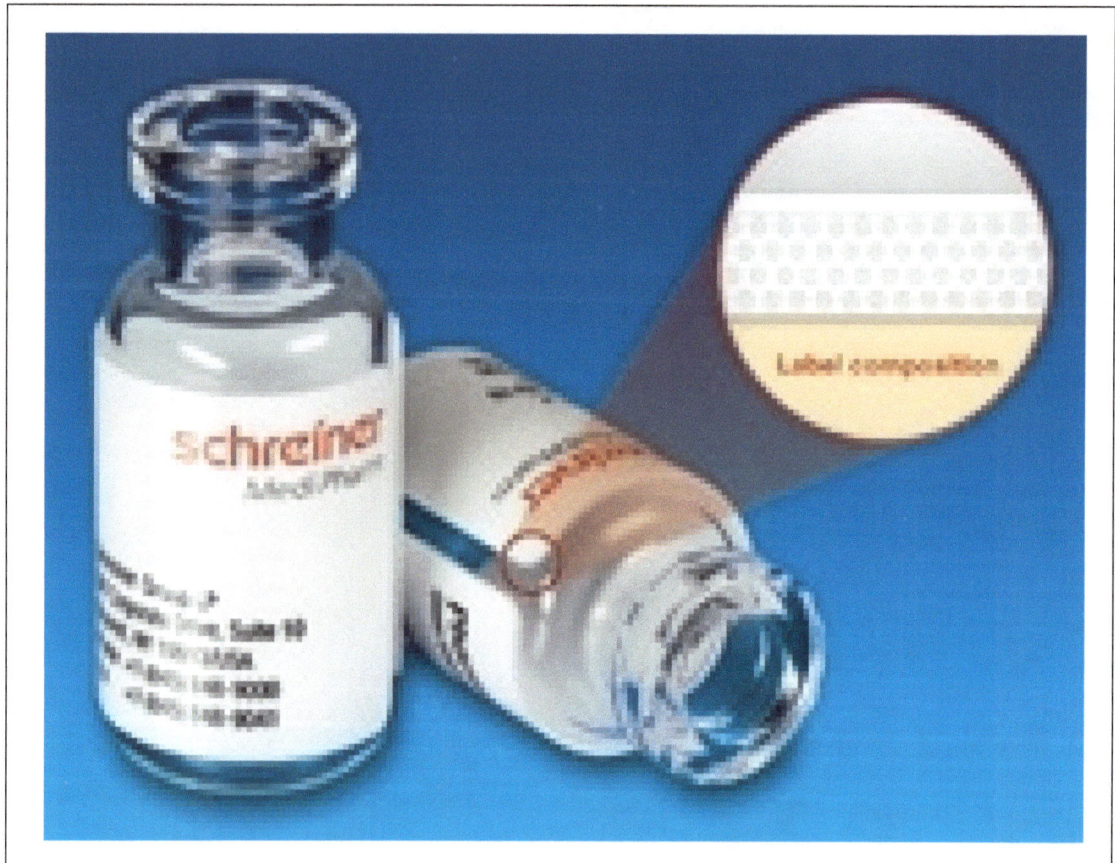

Label composition

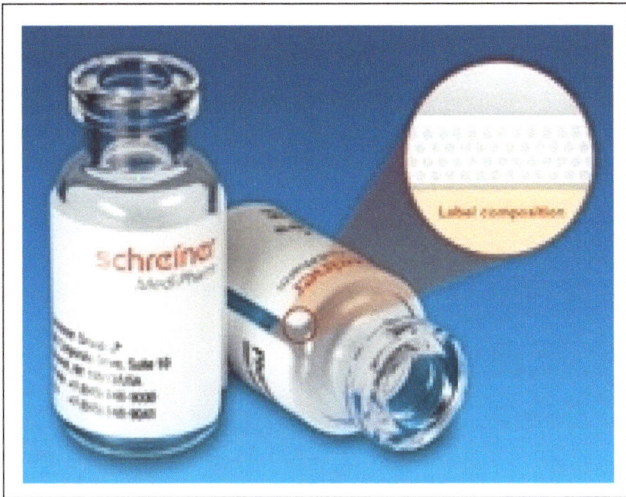

Label composition

Manufacturer/Designer

**Schreiner MediPharm a business unit
of Schreiner Group GmbH & Co. KG
Bruckmannring 22 , 85764 Oberschleißheim "Germany"
Phone: +49 89 31584-5400
Fax: +49 89 31584-5422
E-Mail : info@schreiner-medipharm.com**

Sophisticated labels can offer special functionalities while decreasing the environmental footprint and helping to ensure drug and patient safety

Padded label designed to protect glass vials during processing and shipping

Pharma-Cushion label has a layer of foam on the label's reverse side that wraps around glass containers, which helps minimize the risk of damage while being processed or during transport

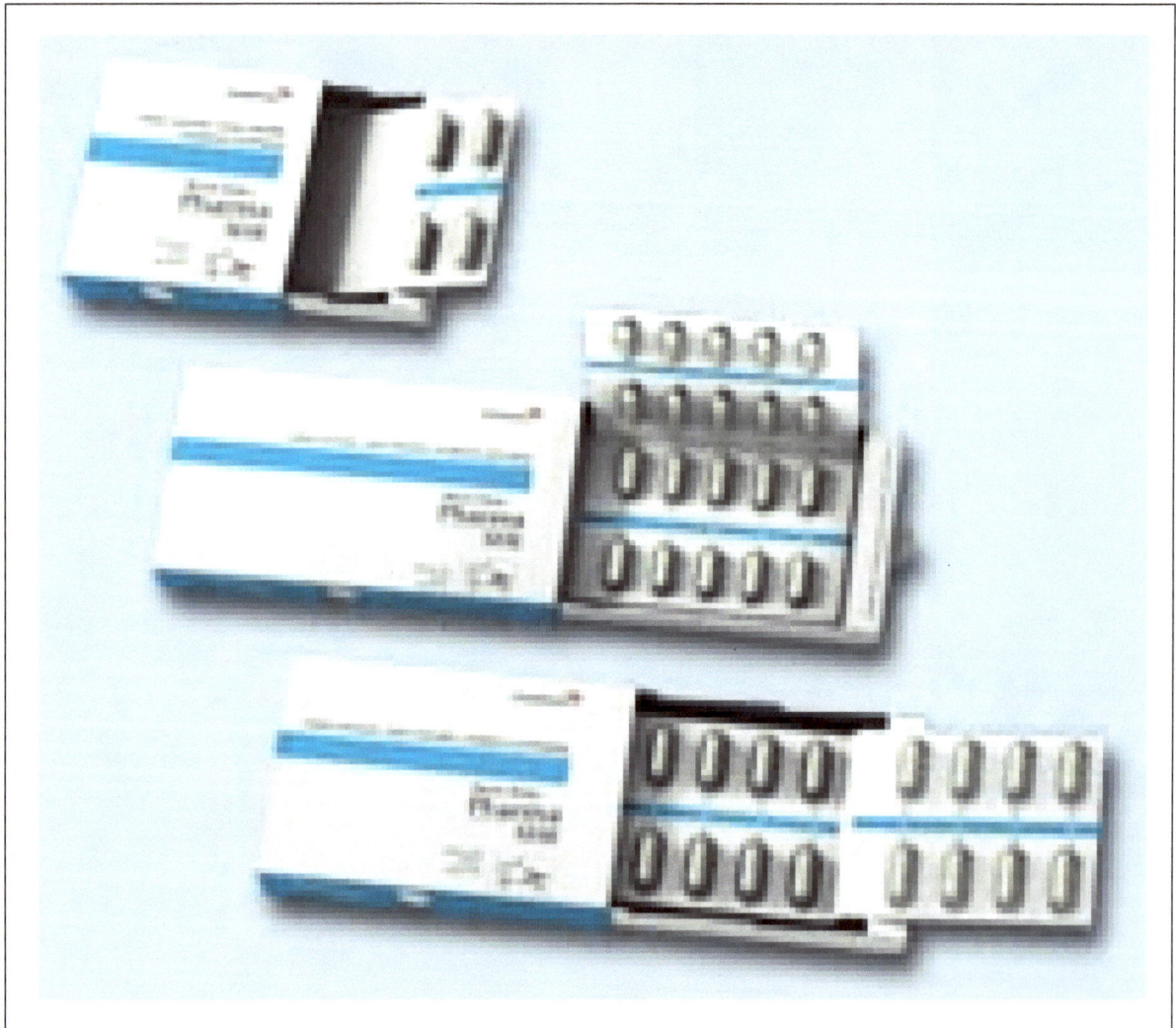

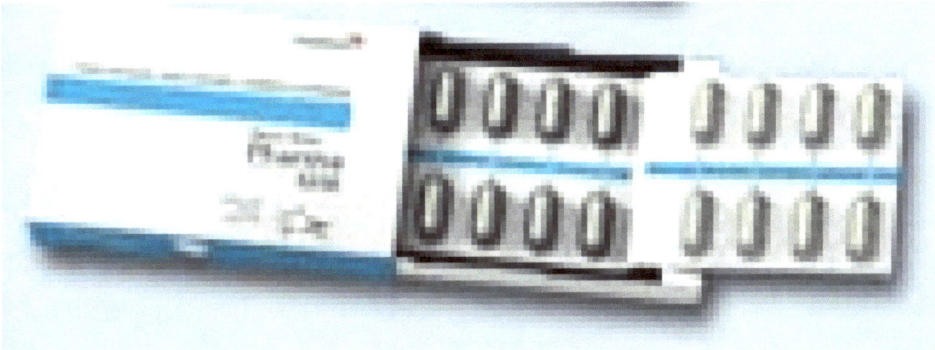

Manufacturer/Designer

rlc | packaging group"Germany"
Phone: +49 511/16499-49
www.rlc-packaging.com

SHR stands for "small hands resistant".

It is a childproof packaging solution made of tear-resistant board that is also easy for the elderly to use.

The opening mechanism is adapted to the hand size of adults and can be opened merely by applying pressure and sliding it.

There is therefore no need to additionally secure the blister cards, wallets or other components inside, which saves materials and work.

This makes the concept ideal for high-dosage medications calling for enhanced protection from children

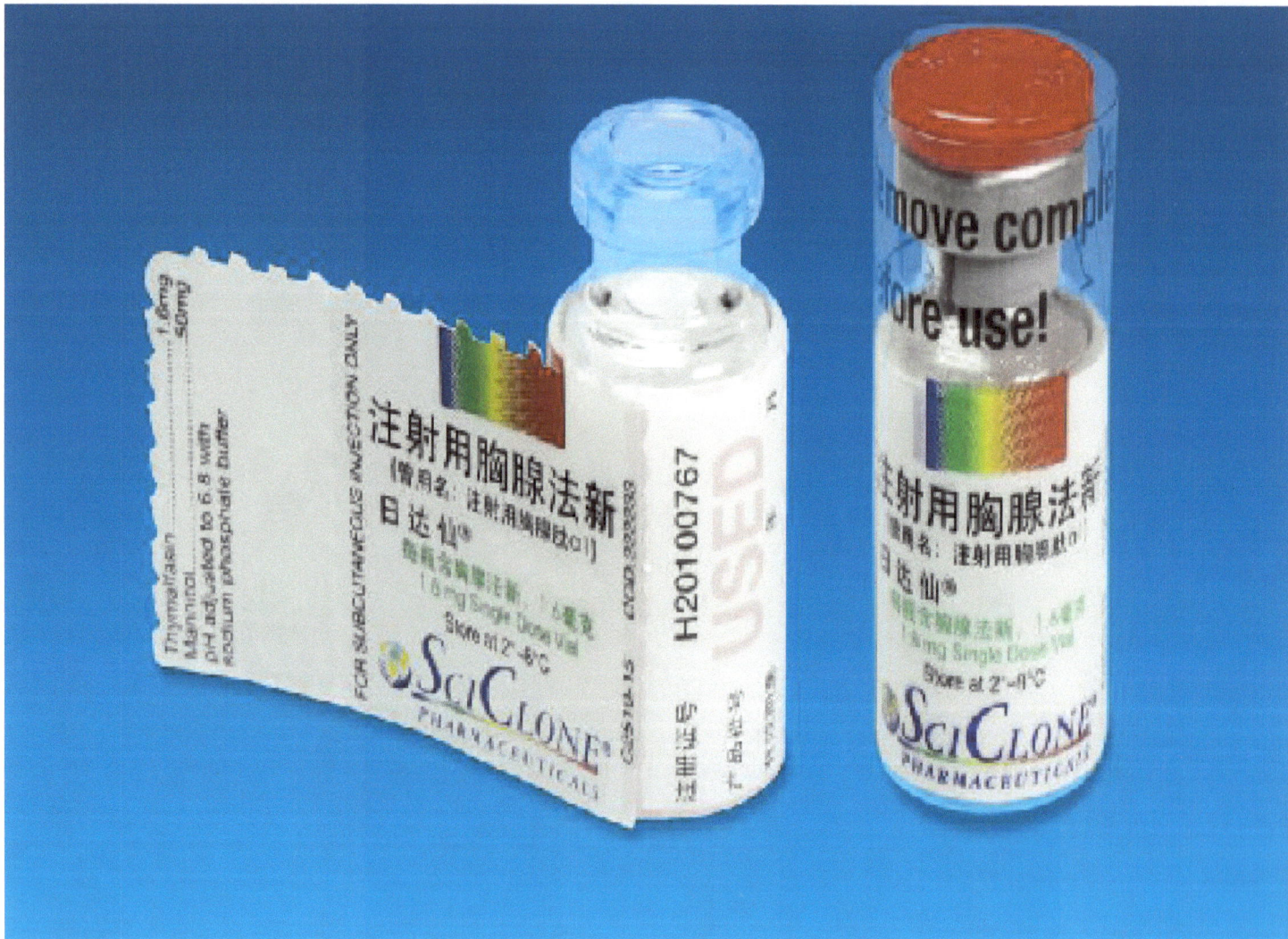

Manufacturer/Designer

Schreiner MediPharm a business unit of
Schreiner Group GmbH & Co. KG
Bruckmannring 22, 85764
Oberschleißheim "Germany"
Phone: +49 89 31584-5400
Fax: +49 89 31584-5422
E-Mail: info@schreiner-medipharm.com

Pharma-Comb Void label's concept for product security

To counteract the practice of refilling previously used medicine vials, the multi-part product label includes integrated security features

The label is functionally destroyed during its initial use.

When the label's tear strip, which also runs around the closure cap, is removed, the inscriptions "Opened" and "Used" appear in the film's two indicator fields.

PHARMA PACKAGING INNOVATIONS

Enjoy Wonders of Packaging!